GLOBAL ECONOMIC STUDIES

U.S. TRADE, PROTECTIONISM AND THE GLOBAL ECONOMIC DOWNTURN

GLOBAL ECONOMIC STUDIES

Additional books in this series can be found on Nova's website at:

https://www.novapublishers.com/catalog/index.php?cPath=23_29&seriesp=Global+Economic+Studies

Additional e- books in this series can be found on Nova's website at:

https://www.novapublishers.com/catalog/index.php?cPath=23_29&seriespe=Global+Economic+Studies

GLOBAL ECONOMIC STUDIES

U.S. TRADE, PROTECTIONISM AND THE GLOBAL ECONOMIC DOWNTURN

ANDREW J. CALDWELL
EDITOR

Nova Science Publishers, Inc.
New York

For permission to use material from this book please contact us:
Telephone 631-231-7269; Fax 631-231-8175
Web Site: http://www.novapublishers.com

LIBRARY OF CONGRESS CATALOGING-IN-PUBLICATION DATA

Available Upon Request

ISBN : 978-1-60876-966-7

Published by Nova Science Publishers, Inc. ✢ New York

CONTENTS

PREFACE

The U.S. trade deficit is shrinking primarily because the global financial crisis is causing U.S. exports to drop faster than U.S. imports. In today's severe global economic downturn, concerns are being raised that countries may try to improve their own trade positions in order to help domestic industries at the expense of others by imposing measures that artificially increase their exports or restrict imports. Such efforts are considered by some to be a form of "protectionism". This book develops three scenarios to approximate different dimensions of the relationship between the global economic downturn and protectionism, as well as reviewing why the U.S. trade deficit is shrinking so severely.

Chapter 1 - In the globalized world of business, production is becoming fragmented into discrete activities and can be spread geographically within and across national borders while remaining integrated organizationally within a multinational company or network of companies. Such globalized production networks are called supply chains or value-added networks. This world of supply chains raises both challenges and opportunities for U.S. policymakers, firms, and workers.

The globalization of production networks has raised policy issues and has called into question certain long-held perceptions about the efficacy and effects of policy initiatives. Traditional trade and investment policy is based on national governments, national economies, and country-to-country relations, but much of trade today is between related companies spread across the globe. How does protecting or promoting one domestic industry affect other parts of its or other supply chains? How does the United States ensure the security and integrity of products assembled offshore from components that are procured from a variety of markets around the world? How does policy affect the competitiveness of U.S.-based businesses in the global marketplace?

Congressional interest in this issue stems from the essential American interests of economic well-being, security, and the projection of values as well as the constitutional mandate for Congress to regulate commerce with foreign nations. Congress also deals with a variety of policies related to investments and capital flows, market access, currency misalignment, intellectual property rights, product safety, shipping security, labor, and the environment. In a broader sweep, the globalization of business strikes directly at issues related to maintaining the U.S. industrial base, the education and training of the American labor force, immigration, health care, and myriad other factors that determine the well-being of Americans.

In international trade, traditional policies aimed at reducing border barriers still tend to increase economic efficiency, but global supply chains may affect the incidence or impact of the policies. Raising import barriers in the United States on products from China, for example, may increase costs for Chinese exporters, but they also have a parallel effect on U.S. multinational companies with manufacturing operations in China that ship to the United States. In fiscal policy, globalized supply chains affect the "multiplier effect" of government policies to stimulate the economy. In shipping security policies, a distinct trade-off exists between greater security and shipping costs. A variety of government policies, both at the national and state level, affect the ability of businesses to compete in the international marketplace and the incentive to locate in the U.S. market. These include tax, labor, environmental, infrastructure, and education policies.

A possible test for policy is to ask if the predominant effect is one of diversion or creation. Does a proposed policy divert production from the U.S. economy to a foreign location, draw production toward a U.S.-based location, or shift production between two foreign locations? Does the proposed policy create more production, or does it discourage productive activity? Does the policy encourage job creation in the United States or does it induce firms to shift jobs overseas? Does the policy disrupt or enhance supply chain operations and decrease or increase overall supply chain efficiency and profitability? And perhaps most fundamentally, how can policy be fashioned to encourage the retention of jobs in the United States while keeping U.S. firms internationally competitive in a complex and globalized world?

The 2008 world financial crisis has demonstrated that the forces of globalization[1] have affected two major parts of the world economy: the global financial system and the global production system. These financial and real (goods-and-services producing) sectors are closely interconnected and synergistically intertwined. The financial crisis demonstrated that the combination of globalization, new technology, new financial instruments, and unrecognized risks, can cause major upheavals in markets that can spread from firm to firm and then from country to country.

In this globalized world, production is becoming more fragmented into discrete activities and can be spread geographically within and across national borders while remaining integrated organizationally within a multinational company or network of companies. This report begins with an overview of global supply chains, why they have developed, and how the variables in the chain (including government policy) relate to each other. It then examines the types of policies that affect different parts of the global supply network and concludes with a discussion of policy review mechanisms. In any global supply structure, there are trade-offs between border transaction costs (including tariffs), factor costs (including labor and capital), logistical costs (including shipping), costs of quality control, external business costs (ease of doing business, regulations, etc.), and various risks (including financial and political risk). Government economic policy often affects each of these tradeoffs in different ways.

Globalized manufacturing chains relate directly to the two main national interests of the United States, security and economic well-being, and relate indirectly to the third—the projection of American values. On the security side, the constant flow of imports streaming into U.S. ports and through border crossings raises the potential for illicit or dangerous cargo, including possible terrorist devices, to enter the United States. On the economic well-being side, the globalized supply chains represent changes in crucial segments of the U.S. economy that ultimately affect the well being of Americans. They bring into play fundamental economic issues such as jobs, wage levels, income distribution, entrepreneurship, and the profitability of businesses. At a more basic level, U.S. manufacturers and providers of services form the foundation of the economy and generate the resources available to support the well-being of Americans, governmental activities, and the ability of the nation to pursue its security and other national interests.

As for the projection of American values, globalization and the economic opportunities it generates, can raise standards of living in countries, such as China or Vietnam, and thereby can potentially create alternative centers of power and channels of communication that may challenge repressive governments or help in resolving problems with democracy, the rule of law, and human rights. However, globalized supply chains also may provide resources for certain repressive governments or, in the case of China, help in providing a rationale for the ruling party to continue its dominance. The presence of U.S. or other international corporations in countries may provide a mechanism for U.S. business and labor practices, as well as language, culture, and values to be spread to other parts of the local populations. Foreign investors, however, may be attracted to authoritarian governments because they tend to create stability even though that stability may be at the sacrifice of certain freedoms or human rights. The globalization of manufacturing also is creating dependency and interaction among trading partners, such as China and Japan or China and Taiwan. These seem to be ameliorating historical friction points and promoting stability in regions. For certain countries, such as China, the nation's increased economic influence, generated partly from their crucial role in global supply chains, has provided Beijing with greater voice in international fora and arguably some leverage in negotiations with the United States.

The globalization of production networks and supply chains also has raised policy questions and has called into question certain long-held perceptions about the efficacy and effects of policy initiatives. For example, a large proportion of international trade is conducted within production networks and chains that cross international borders. How does this affect traditional trade and investment policy that is based on national governments, national economies, and country-tocountry relations? How have global supply chains affected American jobs? How does the United States ensure the security and integrity of products assembled offshore from components that are procured from a variety of markets around the world? Other policy issues include how to target fiscal policy to generate the largest possible beneficial effects, the degree to which the government should act to retain industries and related job opportunities in the United States, the extent to which American jobs are being "outsourced" overseas, the role of U.S. policy in promoting overseas investment, competition by governments (including state governments) to attract foreign investment, and the arguably declining manufacturing base in the United States.

Congressional interest in this issue stems from the aforementioned national interests as well as its constitutional mandate to regulate commerce with foreign nations. Congress also deals with the variety of policies that arise with respect to international trade, import competition, investments and capital flows, market access, currency misalignment, intellectual property rights, product safety, shipping security, labor, and the environment. In a broader sweep, the globalization of business strikes directly at issues related to maintaining the U.S. industrial base, the education and training of the American labor force, health care, and the myriad other factors that determine the level of competitiveness of U.S.-based business in international commerce.

U.S. public policies combine with business costs and other factors to affect the shape, geographical location, and operation of supply chains. Conversely, the existence of supply chains may affect U.S. policymaking. Trade policy aimed at curbing imports from China, for example, would likely affect Chinese exporters and ancillary sectors, but it also may hit subsidiaries of U.S. companies and manufacturers whose supply chains stretch there. It is not surprising, therefore, that some of the strongest voices both for and against trade protectionism come from American- based manufacturers and service providers.

A crucial issue for U.S. policymakers is how to create conditions that make the U.S. economy more attractive as a location for both U.S. parented supply chains and for segments of supply chains of foreign companies. This directly affects job creation for Americans. A possible test for policy is to ask if the predominant effect is diversion or creation. Does the policy divert production from the U.S. economy to a foreign location, draw production toward a U.S.-based location, or shift production between two foreign locations? Does the proposed policy create more production? Does it induce foreign businesses to locate segments of their supply chains here? Does it create jobs in the United States or merely shift them from one foreign country to another? What effect does the policy have on supply chain operations, efficiency, profitability and the distribution of benefits between labor and management?

As the 111th Congress and the new Administration consider changes to economic policy, the basic issues raised by global supply chains may come into play, particularly considerations of the incidence of policies. For example, is the goal of a policy to support business to promote the overall efficiency and profitability of U.S. parented supply chains even if significant segments of those chains are located abroad, or is the goal to induce companies to move production or other business activity to the United States even if such action reduces supply chain efficiency and the ability of the U.S.-parented supply chain to compete in the global marketplace? In international trade and investment policies, does the incidence of the policy fall on overseas segments of American parented supply chains? If the policy is to reduce imports into the United States, what effect will that have on global supply chain operations? Is there a balance between trade policies designed to increase U.S. exports (e.g., by reducing tariffs abroad) and those that may induce U.S. companies to move production overseas (e.g., easing foreign country limits on direct investments). As global supply chains attempt to maximize their efficiency and profitability, they face trade-offs between border transaction costs (including tariffs), factor costs (including labor and capital), logistical costs (including shipping), external business costs (ease of doing business, regulations, etc.), and various risks (including security, financial, and political risk). How does government economic policy influence these factors and trade-offs in ways that are in accord with, rather than counter to U.S. national goals?

Some of the legislation related to global supply chains in the 111th Congress include a bill condemning the People's Republic of China for its socially unacceptable business practices, including the manufacturing and exportation of unsafe products, casual disregard for the environment, and exploitative employment practices (H.Res. 44 [Poe]); Retooling America's Workers for a Green Economy Act (S. 269[Murray]); Achievement Through Technology and Innovation Act of 2009 (H.R. 558 [Roybal-Allard]); Trade Enforcement Act of 2009 (H.R. 496 [Rangel]); 10,000 Trained by 2010 Act (H.R. 461 [Wu]); or Strengthening Our Economy Through Small Business Innovation Act of 2009 (S. 177 [Feingold]).

The 110th Congressed passed the Consumer Product Safety Improvement Act of 2008 that reformed the Consumer Product Safety Commission and strengthened enforcement of consumer product safety standards (H.R. 4040 [Rush, P.L. 110-3 14])[2] and the America Competes Act that promotes investment in science and engineering research and in science, technology, engineering, and mathematics education (H.Res. 602/H.R. 2272 [Sutton, P.L. 110-69]).

Chapter 2 - In today's severe global economic downturn, concerns are being raised that countries may try to improve their own trade positions in order to help domestic industries at the expense of others by imposing measures that artificially increase their exports or restrict imports. Such efforts are considered by some to be a form of "protectionism" and are often referred to as beggar-thyneighbor policies.

This report develops three scenarios to approximate different dimensions of the relationship between the global economic downturn and protectionism. The scenarios are not predictions, but descriptions of how and why pressures for protection could be manifested and transmitted under different circumstances and assumptions.

Under a **low impact scenario,** existing World Trade Organization (WTO) rules and obligations, bolstered by a high level of global interdependence, discourage trade restrictions and trade diverting measures from being proposed. If implemented, the measures conform to WTO rules and/or have a limited impact on trade flows. Recent reports issued by the WTO and World Bank provide preliminary support for this scenario.

Under a **medium impact scenario,** WTO rules are violated or are disregarded due to the exigencies of the economic crisis and demands to provide financial rescue plans for the banking and auto sectors. As a result, trade and investment flows over time could be diverted or fall outside WTO surveillance, thereby weakening the global trading system.

Under a **high impact scenario,** WTO rules are violated, major trade conflict occurs, and the world trading system is undermined. This threat arises from the longstanding presence of large trade imbalances driven by distorted global consumption and savings patterns—patterns that were an underlying cause of the global economic downturn. Given the prominent role that China and the United States play in the global imbalances, two flashpoints for any outbreak of protectionism can be identified. The first could stem from U.S. public concerns that other countries are gaining a "free ride" in terms of international efforts to increase aggregate spending and get the world economy growing again. The second could arise if China and other surplus countries try to avoid massive factory closings and layoffs by exporting their overcapacity to the United States and Europe with trade policy measures such as export subsidies and currency depreciation.

Three broad policy challenges for Congress are derived from the analysis. The first deals with international surveillance of fiscal stimulus programs. The second relates to multilateral surveillance of trade pressures and barriers proposed and adopted during the economic crisis. The third pertains to the joint management of U.S. trade relations by Congress and the administration, particularly as it bears on responding to constituent requests for protection, facilitating the adjustment of current account surplus countries, and formulating trade liberalization priorities.

Chapter 3 - The U.S. trade deficit is shrinking primarily because the global financial crisis is causing U.S. imports to drop faster than U.S. exports. The global simultaneous recession, however, implies that exporting countries cannot rely on increased foreign demand to make up for slack demand at home. Even though U.S. imports are projected to decline, companies competing with imports are still likely to face diminishing demand as the domestic economy shrinks. These conditions imply that the political forces to protect domestic industry from imports are likely to intensify both in the United States and abroad.

In 2008, the **trade deficit in goods** reached $821.2 billion on a balance of payments (BoP) basis, up slightly from $819.4 billion in 2007 but less than the $838.3 billion in 2006. The 2008 deficit on merchandise trade with China was $266.3 billion (Census basis), with the European Union was $93.4 billion, with Japan was $72.7 billion, with Canada was $74.2 billion, with Mexico was $64.4 billion, and the Asian Newly Industrialized Countries (Hong Kong, South Korea, Singapore, and Taiwan) was $3.8 billion. **Imports of goods** of $2,112.5 billion increased by $144.7 billion (7.3%) over 2007. **Exports of goods** of $1,291.3 billion rose by $142.8 billion (12.4%). Although the overall trade deficit for 2008 was up, in the fourth quarter as the U.S. recession worsened, imports declined faster than exports resulting in a trade deficit for the month of December that was $23.0 billion less than the comparable deficit for July.

Trade deficits are a concern for Congress because they may generate trade friction and pressures for the government to do more to open foreign markets, to shield U.S. producers from foreign competition, or to assist U.S. industries to become more competitive. Overall U.S. trade deficits reflect excess spending (a shortage of savings) in the domestic economy and a reliance on capital imports to finance that shortfall. Capital inflows serve to offset the outflow of dollars used to pay for imports. Movements in the exchange rate help to balance trade. The rising trade deficit (when not matched by capital inflows) places downward pressure on the value of the dollar which, in turn, helps to shrink the deficit by making U.S. exports cheaper and imports more expensive. Central banks in countries such as China, however, have intervened in foreign exchange markets to keep the value of their currencies from rising too fast.

The broadest measure of U.S. international economic transactions is the balance on current account. In addition to merchandise trade, it includes trade in services and unilateral transfers. In 2007, the deficit on current account fell to a revised $738.6 billion from a revised $811.5 billion in 2006. In trade in advanced technology products, the U.S. balance improved from a deficit of $38 billion in 2006 but deteriorated to $53 billion in 2007 and $56 billion in 2008. In trade in motor vehicles and parts, the $107 billion U.S. deficit in 2007 was mainly with Japan, Mexico, Germany, and South Korea. In crude oil, major sources of the $342 billion in imports were Canada, Saudi Arabia, Venezuela, Nigeria, and Mexico. This report will be updated periodically.

In: U.S. Trade, Protectionism and the Global... ISBN: 978-1-60876-966-7
Editors: Andrew J. Caldwell

Chapter 1

GLOBALIZED SUPPLY CHAINS AND U.S. POLICY

Dick K. Nanto

SUMMARY

In the globalized world of business, production is becoming fragmented into discrete activities and can be spread geographically within and across national borders while remaining integrated organizationally within a multinational company or network of companies. Such globalized production networks are called supply chains or value-added networks. This world of supply chains raises both challenges and opportunities for U.S. policymakers, firms, and workers.

The globalization of production networks has raised policy issues and has called into question certain long-held perceptions about the efficacy and effects of policy initiatives. Traditional trade and investment policy is based on national governments, national economies, and country-to-country relations, but much of trade today is between related companies spread across the globe. How does protecting or promoting one domestic industry affect other parts of its or other supply chains? How does the United States ensure the security and integrity of products assembled offshore from components that are procured from a variety of markets around the world? How does policy affect the competitiveness of U.S.-based businesses in the global marketplace?

Congressional interest in this issue stems from the essential American interests of economic well-being, security, and the projection of values as well as the constitutional mandate for Congress to regulate commerce with foreign nations. Congress also deals with a variety of policies related to investments and capital flows, market access, currency misalignment, intellectual property rights, product safety, shipping security, labor, and the environment. In a broader sweep, the globalization of business strikes directly at issues related to maintaining the U.S. industrial base, the education and training of the American labor force, immigration, health care, and myriad other factors that determine the well-being of Americans.

In international trade, traditional policies aimed at reducing border barriers still tend to increase economic efficiency, but global supply chains may affect the incidence or impact of the policies. Raising import barriers in the United States on products from China, for example, may increase costs for Chinese exporters, but they also have a parallel effect on U.S. multinational companies with manufacturing operations in China that ship to the United States. In fiscal policy, globalized supply chains affect the "multiplier effect" of government policies to stimulate the economy. In shipping security policies, a distinct trade-off exists between greater security and shipping costs. A variety of government policies, both at the national and state level, affect the ability of businesses to compete in the international marketplace and the incentive to locate in the U.S. market. These include tax, labor, environmental, infrastructure, and education policies.

A possible test for policy is to ask if the predominant effect is one of diversion or creation. Does a proposed policy divert production from the U.S. economy to a foreign location, draw production toward a U.S.-based location, or shift production between two foreign locations? Does the proposed policy create more production, or does it discourage productive activity? Does the policy encourage job creation in the United States or does it induce firms to shift jobs overseas? Does the policy disrupt or enhance supply chain operations and decrease or increase overall supply chain efficiency and profitability? And perhaps most fundamentally, how can policy be fashioned to encourage the retention of jobs in the United States while keeping U.S. firms internationally competitive in a complex and globalized world?

The 2008 world financial crisis has demonstrated that the forces of globalization[1] have affected two major parts of the world economy: the global financial system and the global production system. These financial and real (goods-and-services producing) sectors are closely interconnected and synergistically intertwined. The financial crisis demonstrated that the combination of globalization, new technology, new financial instruments, and unrecognized risks, can cause major upheavals in markets that can spread from firm to firm and then from country to country.

In this globalized world, production is becoming more fragmented into discrete activities and can be spread geographically within and across national borders while remaining integrated organizationally within a multinational company or network of companies. This report begins with an overview of global supply chains, why they have developed, and how the variables in the chain (including government policy) relate to each other. It then examines the types of policies that affect different parts of the global supply network and concludes with a discussion of policy review mechanisms. In any global supply structure, there are trade-offs between border transaction costs (including tariffs), factor costs (including labor and capital), logistical costs (including shipping), costs of quality control, external business costs (ease of doing business, regulations, etc.), and various risks (including financial and political risk). Government economic policy often affects each of these tradeoffs in different ways.

Globalized manufacturing chains relate directly to the two main national interests of the United States, security and economic well-being, and relate indirectly to the third—the projection of American values. On the security side, the constant flow of imports streaming into U.S. ports and through border crossings raises the potential for illicit or dangerous cargo, including possible terrorist devices, to enter the United States. On the economic well-being side, the globalized supply chains represent changes in crucial segments of the U.S. economy that ultimately affect the well being of Americans. They bring into play fundamental economic issues such as jobs, wage levels, income distribution, entrepreneurship, and the profitability of businesses. At a more basic level, U.S. manufacturers and providers of services form the foundation of the economy and generate the resources available to support the well-being of Americans, governmental activities, and the ability of the nation to pursue its security and other national interests.

As for the projection of American values, globalization and the economic opportunities it generates, can raise standards of living in countries, such as China or Vietnam, and thereby can potentially create alternative centers of power and channels of communication that may challenge repressive governments or help in resolving problems with democracy, the rule of law, and human rights. However, globalized supply chains also may provide resources for certain repressive governments or, in the case of China, help in providing a rationale for the ruling party to continue its dominance. The presence of U.S. or other international corporations in countries may provide a mechanism for U.S. business and labor practices, as well as language, culture, and values to be spread to other parts of the local populations. Foreign investors, however, may be attracted to authoritarian governments because they tend to create stability even though that stability may be at the sacrifice of certain freedoms or human rights. The globalization of manufacturing also is creating dependency and interaction among trading partners, such as China and Japan or China and Taiwan. These seem to be ameliorating historical friction points and promoting stability in regions. For certain countries, such as China, the nation's increased economic influence, generated partly from their crucial role in global supply chains, has provided Beijing with greater voice in international fora and arguably some leverage in negotiations with the United States.

The globalization of production networks and supply chains also has raised policy questions and has called into question certain long-held perceptions about the efficacy and effects of policy initiatives. For example, a large proportion of international trade is conducted within production networks and chains that cross international borders. How does this affect traditional trade and investment policy that is based on national governments, national economies, and country-tocountry relations? How have global supply chains affected American jobs? How does the United States ensure the security and integrity of products assembled offshore from components that are procured from a variety of markets around the world? Other policy issues include how to target fiscal policy to generate the largest possible beneficial effects, the degree to which the government should act to retain industries and related job opportunities in the United States, the extent to which American jobs are being "outsourced" overseas, the role of U.S. policy in promoting overseas investment, competition by governments (including state governments) to attract foreign investment, and the arguably declining manufacturing base in the United States.

Congressional interest in this issue stems from the aforementioned national interests as well as its constitutional mandate to regulate commerce with foreign nations. Congress also deals with the variety of policies that arise with respect to international trade, import competition, investments and capital flows, market access, currency misalignment, intellectual property rights, product safety, shipping security, labor, and the environment. In a broader sweep, the globalization of business strikes directly at issues related to maintaining the U.S. industrial base, the education and training of the

American labor force, health care, and the myriad other factors that determine the level of competitiveness of U.S.-based business in international commerce.

U.S. public policies combine with business costs and other factors to affect the shape, geographical location, and operation of supply chains. Conversely, the existence of supply chains may affect U.S. policymaking. Trade policy aimed at curbing imports from China, for example, would likely affect Chinese exporters and ancillary sectors, but it also may hit subsidiaries of U.S. companies and manufacturers whose supply chains stretch there. It is not surprising, therefore, that some of the strongest voices both for and against trade protectionism come from American- based manufacturers and service providers.

A crucial issue for U.S. policymakers is how to create conditions that make the U.S. economy more attractive as a location for both U.S. parented supply chains and for segments of supply chains of foreign companies. This directly affects job creation for Americans. A possible test for policy is to ask if the predominant effect is diversion or creation. Does the policy divert production from the U.S. economy to a foreign location, draw production toward a U.S.-based location, or shift production between two foreign locations? Does the proposed policy create more production? Does it induce foreign businesses to locate segments of their supply chains here? Does it create jobs in the United States or merely shift them from one foreign country to another? What effect does the policy have on supply chain operations, efficiency, profitability and the distribution of benefits between labor and management?

As the 111th Congress and the new Administration consider changes to economic policy, the basic issues raised by global supply chains may come into play, particularly considerations of the incidence of policies. For example, is the goal of a policy to support business to promote the overall efficiency and profitability of U.S. parented supply chains even if significant segments of those chains are located abroad, or is the goal to induce companies to move production or other business activity to the United States even if such action reduces supply chain efficiency and the ability of the U.S.-parented supply chain to compete in the global marketplace? In international trade and investment policies, does the incidence of the policy fall on overseas segments of American parented supply chains? If the policy is to reduce imports into the United States, what effect will that have on global supply chain operations? Is there a balance between trade policies designed to increase U.S. exports (e.g., by reducing tariffs abroad) and those that may induce U.S. companies to move production overseas (e.g., easing foreign country limits on direct investments).

As global supply chains attempt to maximize their efficiency and profitability, they face trade-offs between border transaction costs (including tariffs), factor costs (including labor and capital), logistical costs (including shipping), external business costs (ease of doing business, regulations, etc.), and various risks (including security, financial, and political risk). How does government economic policy influence these factors and trade-offs in ways that are in accord with, rather than counter to U.S. national goals?

Some of the legislation related to global supply chains in the 111th Congress include a bill condemning the People's Republic of China for its socially unacceptable business practices, including the manufacturing and exportation of unsafe products, casual disregard for the environment, and exploitative employment practices (H.Res. 44 [Poe]); Retooling America's Workers for a Green Economy Act (S. 269[Murray]); Achievement Through Technology and Innovation Act of 2009 (H.R. 558 [Roybal-Allard]); Trade Enforcement Act of 2009 (H.R. 496 [Rangel]); 10,000 Trained by 2010 Act (H.R. 461 [Wu]); or Strengthening Our Economy Through Small Business Innovation Act of 2009 (S. 177 [Feingold]).

The 110th Congressed passed the Consumer Product Safety Improvement Act of 2008 that reformed the Consumer Product Safety Commission and strengthened enforcement of consumer product safety standards (H.R. 4040 [Rush, P.L. 110-3 14])[2] and the America Competes Act that promotes investment in science and engineering research and in science, technology, engineering, and mathematics education (H.Res. 602/H.R. 2272 [Sutton, P.L. 110-69]).

A New Paradigm

The globalized American economy poses challenges for U.S. trade and regulatory policy. The traditional paradigm for policy was that the American economy consisted of U.S. businesses that operated primarily in the domestic market, hired U.S. workers, and sold to U.S. consumers but with some production either imported or exported. International trade took place between countries according to each nation's competitive and comparative advantage. A trade policy aimed at a particular country had impact on businesses and consumers in that country. Only indirectly would adverse effects rebound to harm U.S. business interests such as when foreign governments retaliated in kind.

The world now has changed. Like a child's neural network, the global economy is constantly organizing and reorganizing itself with new linkages, supply networks, manufacturing chains, and marketing channels that rise in response to market forces and government policies.

This integrated world economy raises both challenges and opportunities for U.S. policymakers. How U.S. policy responds to this new reality directly affects the well-being of Americans. The existing paradigm based on geographical boundaries, country-to-country trade, vertical integration of manufacturing, and retailers acting as market takers rather than as market makers seems to be in need of updating. A new policy paradigm should account for the evolving world of business in which large U.S. manufacturers and providers of services have become part of increasingly complex international chains in which parts and components are made in multiple locations and assembled in others. In the delivery of services, some still require face-to-face contact (e.g., airline travel or food services) but other business services can be delivered through high speed Internet connections (e.g., computer programming, data analysis, customer relations, or ticket sales).

International trade now is less between countries than within a global supply network that may include headquarters, design, branding, and engineering in the United States but manufacturing in China with parts from Singapore, Japan, and the European Union and call center services in India. For example, a U.S. company may make a computer in Shanghai, but it could have been assembled from chips designed in Texas with a motherboard from Taiwan and manufactured according to specifications by the U.S. brand-name holder in California with software from Washington state and shipped through Hong Kong directly to a retailer either in the American market or abroad. The product service department might be located partly in India or the Philippines. Such supply chain relations tend to be long-term with "upstream" processes directly connected to "downstream" activities and both pitfalls and opportunities for policy at various junctures in the supply chain.

One indicator of the extent to which international trade increasingly is being conducted within companies can be seen in data on exports and imports by U.S. multinational companies (MNCs) with affiliated and non-affiliated companies. Note that many non-affiliated companies may belong to a company's supply chain. As shown in **Figure 1**, in 2006, U.S. MNCs exported \$203.4 billion to their foreign affiliated companies and \$328.4 billion to non-affiliated companies. These exports accounted for half of all U.S. exports of goods in that year. U.S. MNCs also imported \$252.2 billion from their foreign affiliated companies and $426.0 from non-affiliates. This accounted for about a third of all U.S. imports. In 2004, U.S. parent MNCs employed 21.4 million people in the United States and 10.0 million abroad in affiliated companies.

Not shown in **Figure 1** are exports by multinational companies of foreign parentage located in the U.S. market. These include companies such as Toyota, Nokia, Seagram, or Bayer. These American subsidiaries comprise key components of foreign supply chains. In 2006, they employed 5 million people in the U.S. economy, exported $195.3 billion and imported $482.4 billion in goods.[3] Their U.S. operations often are part of a far flung global network. For example, in 2007, the operations of Hitachi of Japan included 16,242 employees in 75 companies in North America, 56,305 employees in China, 49,340 in other Asian nations, 9,468 in Europe, and 251,702 employees in Japan.[4]

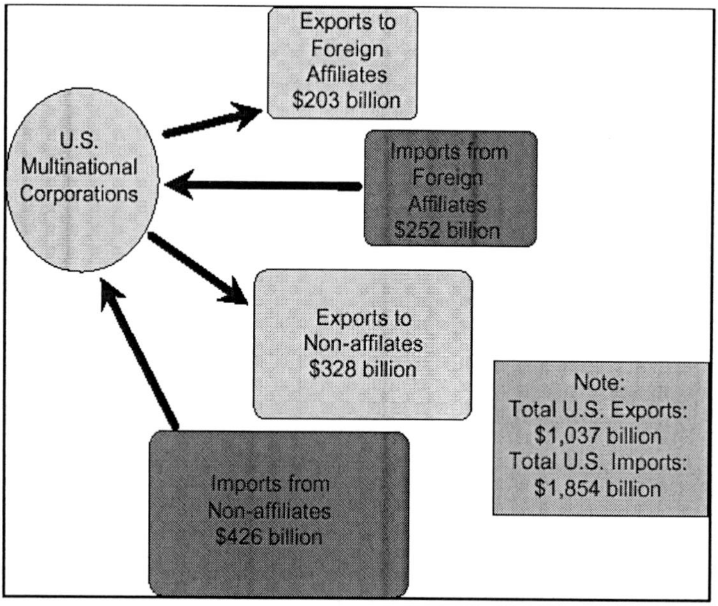

Source: Congressional Research Service. Data from: Raymond J. Mataloni, Jr., "U.S. Multinational Companies, Operations in 2006, "*Survey of Current Business*, November 2008, p.30.

Figure 1. International Trade by U.S. Parent Multinational Companies, 2006

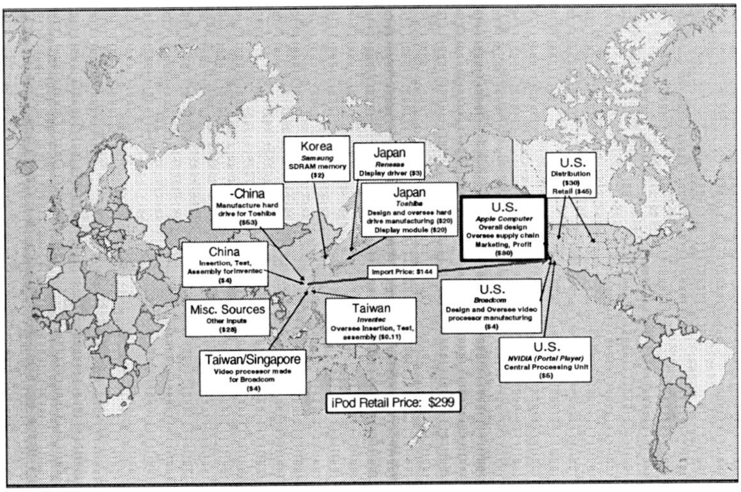

Source: Congressional Research Service. Data from Greg Linden, Kenneth L. Kraemer, Jason Dedrick, "Who Captures Value in a Global Innovation System? The Case of Apple 's iPod, " Personal Computing Industry Center, , June 2007. 10 p. and various other sources.

Figure 2. Manufacturing Supply Chain and Input Costs for the Apple Computer iPod ©in 2005

In a survey on the future of manufacturing undertaken by *Industry Week* magazine in 2008, the U.S. manufacturers that responded indicated that 18% of their products in 2008 were manufactured or directly sourced from outside the United States and that by 2011, they expected 25% would be foreign-sourced. The manufacturers also indicated that 16% of their products in 2008 were being sold outside the United States and that by 2011, they expected 22% would be sold abroad. Of the major regions of the world where companies were sourcing product in 2008, 54% said China, 30% said the European Union, 27% Mexico/Latin America, 22% Southeast Asia, 21% Canada, and 17% said India. Foreign sourcing was expected to increase by 2011 from China, Mexico/Latin America, Southeast Asia, and India but decrease from the European Union and Canada.[5]

One example of a typical supply chain may be that for Apple Computer's iPod music playing device. This is made by a manufacturing chain that stretches across several countries in the Pacific basin. As shown in **Figure 2**, the value of $144 for an iPod imported from China in 2005 had its major parts and services originate from China, the United States, Japan, South Korea, Taiwan, and Singapore.[6] Each of these major components, moreover, may have involved parts from various countries of the world. The iPod supply chain included design, supply chain management, parts production, assembly, shipping, distribution, and retail. Note that less than half of the $299 retail cost is accounted for by the $144 import price. The largest share of the retail price arises from Apple Computer's profit and other activities and in U.S. distribution and retail. Some of the parts also originate from U.S. companies. The supply chain also includes transportation and logistics management, financing, risk management, and quality control. Many of these services may be provided by an American company. Apple Computer also sells iPods in the global marketplace. Although, these may be shipped directly from China, they contain U.S. parts and generate profits for Apple.

In this globalized business world, products may be pushed through the international supply network by an American holder of the brand name, or they may be pulled through the network by a major U.S. retailer. In either case, relevant U.S. policies include those affecting international trade, exchange rates, product safety, shipping security, as well as costs of fuel and raw materials, labor quality and price, and the existence of production infrastructure. These combine to affect the shape, geographical location, and operation of the supply chain. Conversely, the existence of the supply chain may affect U.S. policymaking. Trade policy aimed at curbing imports from China, for example, would likely affect Chinese exporters and ancillary sectors, but it also may hit subsidiaries of U.S. companies and manufacturers whose supply chains stretch there. It is not surprising, therefore, that some of the strongest voices both for and against trade protectionism come from American-based manufacturers and service providers.

The manufacturing sector, moreover, can operate only if it is supported by a robust and capable financial sector. Manufacturing managers tend to focus their energies on producing goods and use financial services companies to handle most financial activities. Many companies rely heavily on banks, brokerage houses, investment funds, and insurance companies to raise capital, finance transactions, insure against risks, and issue stock. When the financial sector is in crisis, the manufacturing sector is usually not far behind. For manufactures, such as General Motors, with in-house financial services, the current financial crisis may have hit them with a dual punch. It may have clobbered both their financial subsidiaries and their sales of product.[7] Trade transactions, moreover, rely heavily on trust and credit. In 2008, thinly capitalized suppliers in other countries were finding it increasingly difficult to obtain new letters of credit. Available loans, moreover, were at higher rates of interest. This was threatening to disrupt the intricate supply chains that reached into China and emerging markets in eastern Europe.[8]

GLOBAL SUPPLY CHAINS: MANUFACTURING IN THE 21ST CENTURY

The commerce clause of the U.S. Constitution ensured that the various state economies would unite into a vast American market allowing for the free movement of goods, capital, and labor anywhere within the nation. As the economy developed, the government intervened to subsidize the building of a transportation infrastructure (roads, railways, ports, and airports) and communication facilities, to regulate business, and to protect intellectual property. This huge, unified market gave U.S. businesses a distinct advantage in global markets because they could spread their operations across multiple state markets and take advantage of concentrations of consumers, natural resource endowments, and different labor skills and wages but still operate under a common federal regulatory system.

Over the past half century, three revolutionary changes have redefined business production methods and spawned the development of globalized supply chains. The first has been the development of low-cost shipping along with fast and cheap communications. The second is business management strategy that calls for a focus on core competencies,[9] just-in-time production,[10] steady improvement in product quality, risk minimization, flexibility in meeting consumer demand, and profit maximization over a supply chain rather than for each entity within that chain. The third is the reduction in international trade and investment barriers worldwide through both multilateral and bilateral trade agreements. These changes have encouraged the globalization of business, but they also may coincide or conflict with national goals of full employment, economic growth, balance in international trade accounts, and national security.

Typical Supply Chains

In the world today, a supply chain exists for almost all products traded in the international marketplace. **Figure 3** illustrates a typical supply chain for furniture companies with headquarters in either the United States or China but with most of the manufacturing done in China with some inputs from the United States. This could be a brand-name furniture chain with headquarters in the United States, or it could be a major retailer that pulls product through its network of suppliers. In 2007, the United States exported $593 million in wood (for all uses) to China and imported $20 billion in furniture. The United States also provided furniture design and branding, distribution, some upholstery fabric, certain machinery and tools, some chemicals, quality control to a certain extent, and some shipping and other logistics as well as U.S. distribution and retail operations.

Where in this supply chain does the United States have an advantage? American companies specialize in high-value added activities such as chemicals, seeds, upholstery design, machinery manufacturing, and the design and advertising of the final product. Abundant natural forests and land also allow the United States to specialize in production of lumber, some of which goes to China. China also procures lumber, particularly hardwoods, from Southeast Asia and Russia. High end furniture that requires customization, skilled woodworking, and is bulky also tends to be manufactured closer to the customer in the United States, and custom cabinetry and wood countertops usually require local manufacture. Still, about half of the mass marketed wood furniture (non-upholstered) market is supplied by imports, and U.S. employment in this sector has fallen by almost half over the 2000-200 5 period. The shift to foreign manufacturing by wood furniture manufacturers and the focus on retail and distribution is highlighted by the change in the name of the "American Furniture Manufacturers Association" to the "American Home Furnishings Alliance."[11] It should be noted, however, that some furniture manufacturing is returning to or being located in the United States. The Swedish firm Ikea has established a production plant in Virginia, and certain high-end brands either are expanding operations in the United States (such as Stickley[12]) or are relocating some production back from overseas to North Carolina (such as La-Z-Boy).[13]

Business Decisions and the Public Interest

In this world of global supply chains, corporate and national interests may coincide with or conflict with each other. For example, a business seeks to minimize costs of production and may turn to lower cost assembly plants abroad while a nation seeks to provide full employment for its citizens. A business seeks continual improvement in the technology and quality embodied in its products and may turn to a foreign manufacturer of a component, while a nation seeks to generate technological change at home. A business seeks to maximize profits and satisfy consumer demand by using a combination of domestic and imported products, while a nation seeks to balance its international trade accounts and to generate economic growth at home.

A fundamental issue is whether the claim still holds that what is good for business is good for the country, and vice versa (this was originally phrased as what is good for General Motors is good for the country.[14]) In an alternative way of stating the problem, Adam Smith postulated in 1776 that individuals seeking their economic self-interest, as if guided by an "invisible hand," actually benefit society more than they would if they tried to benefit society directly.[15] In short, the issue is whether efficiency and profitability for businesses also translate into efficiency and economic well-being for the country as a whole. Do the benefits of greater business efficiency and profitability trickle down to society in general in the form of higher pay and more jobs created?

Supply chains have added complexity to this issue. In the case of Adam Smith's invisible hand or in the statement in 1953 about General Motors, U.S. business referred to companies located in the United States and doing most of their business here. With supply chains, business headquarters may be located in the United States, but production networks may be global. The company usually will attempt to maximize profits and efficiency across the entire supply chain and not just for the domestic part of it. Profits may accrue to the U.S. parent company, but many of the supplier and assembly jobs may be overseas. Whether a policy that is good for business is also good for the United States, therefore, depends on how the profits of business are distributed, how much of the value generated by the business supply chain is created in the United States, and what effect the supply chain has on the U.S. balance of trade and other international accounts.

In establishing a global supply chain, a corporation faces three basic issues. First, what are the core competencies of the company? What part of the manufacturing chain should the company do in-house and what should be contracted out? Second, where should the product be assembled and packaged? Should it be done in the United States, in China, or elsewhere? Third, should the company invest in manufacturing facilities and own the process or rely on suppliers? The outcome of these decisions determine the shape, location, and interconnections within the supply chain.

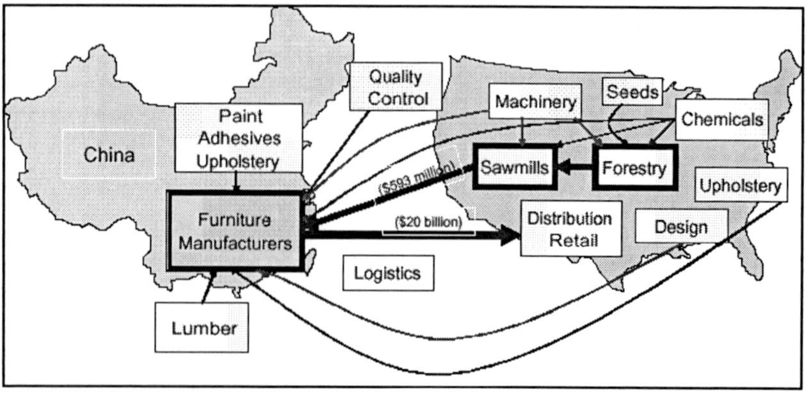

Source: Congressional Research Service

Figure 3. Typical Manufacturing Supply Chain for Wood Furniture from China in 2007

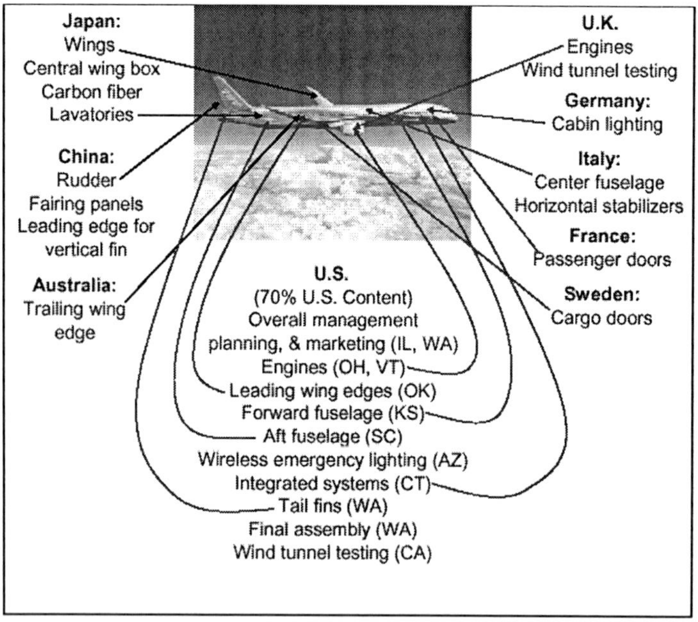

Source: Congressional Research Service from data from “Boeing 787: A Matter of Materials, "Industry Week, December 1,2007,pp.35-37 plus several news articles.Photograph from The Boeing Company.

Figure 4. Major Global Sourcing for the Boeing 787 Dreamliner

For example, the new Boeing 787 Dreamliner passenger aircraft (first deliveries scheduled for 2010) is based on a supply chain that incorporates many business and policy decisions involved in making a complex product. Although final assembly is done near Seattle, Boeing outsources about 70% of the total content of the aircraft (up from about 50% in previous planes) with about 30% of the content outsourced from foreign suppliers.[16] As shown in **Figure 4**, many components and parts of the airplane come from Europe and Asia as well as from the United States. France makes passenger doors; the U.K. provides Rolls Royce engines, Italy the center fuselage and horizontal stabilizers, Sweden cargo doors, Germany the main cabin lighting, Japan wings and the central wing box as well as carbon fiber jointly developed with Boeing, China the rudder and other parts; and Australia provides the trailing wing edge. Since passenger airplanes are purchased by airlines that often are owned by or have close relationships with governments, part of Boeing's marketing strategy is to get major customer nations involved in production to provide them a vested interest in the financial success of the aircraft. Boeing is a leading U.S. exporter, but it does so partly because it also cooperates with potential customer countries in the development and production of aircraft. The U.S. Export-Import Bank also plays a role in funding exports of aircraft.[17]

Boeing's supply chain for the 787 Dreamliner illustrates several of the central tenets of 21st century manufacturing. Boeing focuses on its core competencies (designing, assembling, and marketing airplanes), attempts to maximize efficiency over the entire production network, minimizes inventories through a just-in-time manufacturing process, and works with suppliers to engender technological progress and more exacting quality control. Some of these business goals favor foreign sourcing of production or parts while others favor domestic sources. Some critics of producing wings in Japan, for example, fear that Boeing may be fostering a Japanese aircraft industry that may become a future competitor.[18] Boeing also must consider U.S. and foreign government policies in various aspects of its business decisions.

Many aspects of U.S. public policy support Boeing's production of aircraft. These arguably include procurement by the Department of Defense, the financing of exports through the Export- Import Bank, subsidies for research and development, subsidies for the education and training of engineers and other skilled workers, subsidies for airport construction, and official trade complaints aimed at European government subsidies of Airbus.[19] Boeing is a major U.S. exporter and generates job opportunities for thousands of Americans despite its supply chain that reaches overseas. These imports of parts and components, however, tend to be offset by exports of final product.

The iPod supply chain in **Figure 2** represents a corporate network that is a net importer. The production of iPods or similar consumer electronics also may benefit from U.S. government policies. These may include government procurement, the financing of trade transactions, subsidies for research and development, subsidies for aerospace activities (including satellite launches) and the Internet, various government market-opening initiatives, and efforts at strengthening the protection of intellectual property.

Critics of globalization tend to focus on lower costs (because of lower wages or less stringent environmental or other regulations) of manufacturing abroad. For supply chains, however, production decisions can not rest solely on calculations of cost. Cost calculations are combined with estimates of risk to produce expected values for future operations. For example, in deciding whether to assemble a product in China, the risk of currency appreciation, shipping disruptions, political turmoil, changes in Chinese government policy, differential rates of inflation, miscommunication, accidents, terrorist incidents, and other such factors also enter into the calculations. In addition, measures for long-distance quality control and product safety come into play.

For example, the pharmaceutical company Pfizer is undergoing a massive overhaul of its manufacturing and supply network worldwide. Pfizer Global Manufacturing currently supplies more than 500 products with 100 manufacturing plants that it is whittling down to 43. Some plants have been closed, some sold outright, and others sold with trailing supply agreements. Now the company manufactures internally when that makes sense, and it buys the rest from outside sources. The company says that their decisions are not based entirely on cost but on creating value for its customers. This includes cost, quality, reliability, and the speed of product development as well as supply chain security.[20]

THE PUBLIC POLICY DIMENSION OF GLOBAL SUPPLY CHAINS

A crucial issue for U.S. policymakers is how to create conditions that make the U.S. economy more attractive as a location for both headquarters of supply chains and for each segment of both U.S. and foreign parented supply chains. In general, the more value that is added domestically, the more domestic job opportunities that may be created and greater the well-being of Americans. A possible test for policy is to ask if the predominant effect is one of diversion or creation. Does a proposed policy divert production (including services, research, and marketing) and employment that goes with production from the U.S. economy to a foreign location, draw production toward a U.S.-based location, or shift production between two foreign locations? Does the proposed policy create more production, or does it discourage productive activity? Does it induce foreign-owned businesses to locate segments of their supply chains here? Does the policy disrupt or enhance supply chain operations and decrease or increase overall supply chain efficiency and profitability? How does a policy affect the distribution of benefits among corporate executives, workers, shareholders, and consumers? Does a proposed policy encourage the delivery of products for consumers that are high in quality yet low in price? Also, does a proposed policy affect where intellectual property is created or resides, and what are the spinoff benefits for the rest of society?

Public policy affects businesses in two distinct ways. The first is in the environment for business or the economic, political, and social crucible in which it operates. This includes a wide range of factors including basic institutions of private property, commercial law and rights, market access, rights of establishment, national treatment, border barriers, exchange rate policy, protection of intellectual property, infrastructure, education and training of workers, energy policy, the climate for innovation, political governance, and the panoply of policies aimed at the general climate for business that all companies face.

The second way that public policy affects business is in actions that affect the internal operations of companies. These are actions that directly affect costs of production and profitability, and may include tax policy, specific customs duties, wage and employment policies, accounting and reporting rules, health and safety requirements, specific environmental requirements, and product safety. Some policies affecting the general business environment, such as energy costs and subsidies for research and development, also affect internal costs.

The development of global supply chains adds another dimension to the impact of public policy. This appears in the incidence (who is affected) by policy. Since manufacturing processes now have become fractured, the incidence of policy likewise has become fractured. A supply chain consists of a domestic parent, domestic suppliers, foreign suppliers, and a community of supporting functions that include logistics, supply chain management, and quality assurance. Public policy may provide incentives or disincentives for supply chain parent companies to establish and retain their headquarters in the U.S. market. This applies both to historically American companies and to foreign companies that may locate regional headquarters in the United States. Public policies favorable to business in the United States also may induce both American and foreign-owned supply chains to locate more segments of their supply chains in the United States (and vice versa).

U.S. policies, however, also may lower the costs of manufacturing abroad. Reciprocal tariff reductions; free trade areas; reducing market access barriers in other countries; improving U.S. seaports, airports, and other freight handling infrastructure; promoting faster and more efficient communications networks; and certain tax provisions may increase the incentive to source from abroad or to invest in business operations there. While such policies may work counter to efforts to induce businesses to locate activities in the United States, they also may increase the overall profitability of a U.S. parented global supply chain and may better enable U.S. businesses to leverage their supply chain operations in order to sell product in the foreign market. Therefore, while U.S. efforts at decreasing border barriers abroad tend to have an unequivocally positive impact on U.S. economic well-being by increasing U.S. exports, efforts at improving the business environment in foreign countries (such as protecting intellectual property or easing restrictions on foreign investment) tend to have a dual impact. While such efforts may encourage the location of segments of a supply chain in foreign countries, they also may increase the profitability of the supply chain operations for the U.S. parent company. An analogous argument holds for a policy such as imposing additional import tariffs in the United States. While such a policy may increase the incentive to locate production in the U.S. market, it also may reduce the profitability and competitiveness of supply chain operations for U.S. companies. As a result, the chain as a whole may be less able to compete with other global supply chains, may lose business, and may end up with fewer American employees overall.

The proliferation of global supply chains, therefore, has exacerbated certain trade-offs with respect to the effect or incidence of policies. For a given policy proposal, is the larger effect on the supply chain parent, on overseas operations that also affect the parent company, or on company operations, both domestic and foreign, in the United States? The varying effects of the policy may cause seemingly contradictory reactions to policy initiatives. It should not be a surprise to find various interest groups, even those within certain business sectors, at odds with each other. In view of these disparate responses, business associations, such as the National Association of Manufacturers, tend to take positions only on issues of general interest to their members. They usually do not speak out on industry sectoral issues, unless such issues are non-controversial or have wide member support.[21]

Public policy, therefore, affects different segments of the supply chain in different ways. A policy aimed at increasing the number of scientists and engineers in the U.S. economy may help to retain the research and development segment in the United States, but the focus on such high-level skills may lessen the number of new graduates who are willing to take jobs that require only lower- level labor skills and face work processes that tend to be repetitive. A policy aimed at keeping out certain types of imported materials, such as carbon steel, to assist the domestic steel industry may lessen the competitiveness of the automobile and other industries that use steel in their assembly process. The fracturing of the manufacturing process and the outsourcing of components of that process to foreign suppliers, therefore, implies that public policy also may need to be fractured (multidimensional and discriminating), designed to have different effects on different segments of the production chains and the workforce associated with those production activities.

One example of how public policy may enter into business decision making to determine where to manufacture product is an analytical tool reportedly used by Dow Chemical. Dow has manufacturing capacity in several countries and can move production from location to location on short notice. The company has used a linear programming model[22] that takes account of international differences in exchange rates, tax rates, and transportation and labor costs to determine the best mix of production by location for each planning period.[23] The company is able to respond quickly to government policies that may affect exchange rates, taxes, or other cost factors.

In policies aimed at creating a favorable climate for business in the American market, the United States seems to do quite well, Measures of general business climate usually place the United States first in the world in terms of "competitiveness." Relative competitiveness, however, is difficult to measure and metrics tend to be quite general. The measures do, however, indicate how a country compares with other nations as a potential generator of economic growth and as a host for international business. For example, the World Economic Forum publishes the Global Competitiveness Index for 134 countries.[24] Under this index in 2008, the United States ranked first, Switzerland second, Denmark third, Sweden fourth, Germany fifth, Finland sixth, Singapore seventh, Japan, eighth, United Kingdom ninth, and the Netherlands tenth. China was 34th.[25]

Likewise, the Institute for Management Development in Lasuanne, Switzerland publishes a *World Competitiveness Scoreboard* each year that "analyzes the factors and policies that shape the ability of a nation to create and maintain an environment that sustains more value creation for its enterprises and more prosperity for its people." The analysis divides the national environments of 55 countries into four main factors (with 331 criteria): economic performance, government efficiency, business efficiency, and infrastructure. The 2008 scorecard placed the United States first, Singapore second, Hong Kong third, Switzerland fourth, and Luxembourg fifth. China was number 17.[26] According to these analyses, the United States leads the world in providing an economic environment favorable for business.

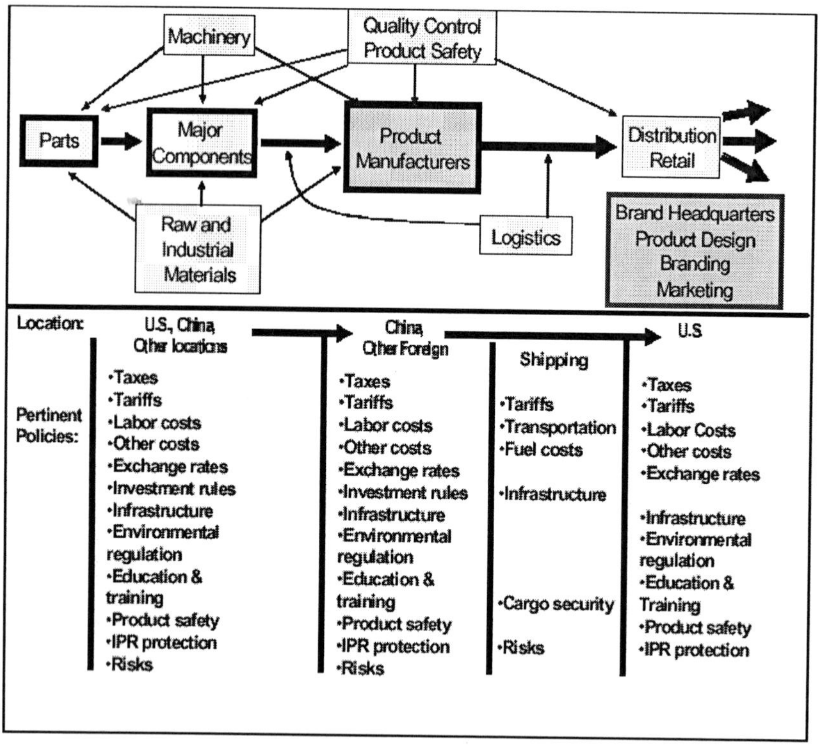

Source: Congressional Research Service

Figure 5. A Typical Global Supply Chain with Pertinent Policy Levers

These comparative indices however, tend to examine underlying performance factors that lead to high incomes and business development. While the United States ranks first in both of these international comparisons, they do not explain why companies headquartered in the United States choose to manufacture in countries that rank lower in "competitiveness." This is where supply chains enter the analysis.

Major Policies Affecting Global Supply Chains

The United States pursues a range of economic policies, some industrial in nature, each carrying a package of economic and political justifications. However, in general, Washington relies mainly on monetary and fiscal policy to generate full employment and economic growth, even though the federal government does support specific industries, such as agriculture or aerospace, and occasionally intervenes directly to provide emergency assistance to firms such as AIG, Citigroup, or General Motors and Chrysler. The policies of most concern in this section are microeconomic in nature and affect both the environment for business and the international operations of companies.

Figure 5 illustrates a typical supply chain with manufacturing in China or other country but with brand headquarters and major retailing in the United States. The figure also shows selected public policies that affect decisions within the supply chain, particularly those dealing with where and how each step in the supply chain is accomplished. Other policies also are important to supply chains, but they are beyond the scope of this report (such as health care, workplace regulation, accounting standards, lawsuits and other legal issues, financial regulations, and executive compensation). Much of the analysis of the policies considered, however, also may apply to these policies.

Taxation

The public policies shown in **Figure 5** are not necessarily ranked according to magnitude of effect, but taxes tend to be at the top of any list of issues for international business. Under the current system, U.S. taxes are applied on a worldwide basis to U.S. firms while granting foreign tax credits in order to alleviate double taxation of the same income. In short, multinational corporations pay taxes on their global income but receive credit for taxes paid to foreign governments. The system permits U.S. firms to defer taxes on foreign-source income indefinitely by not repatriating profits. In effect, the current system provides an incentive for companies to retain profits abroad and to invest in low-tax countries and a disincentive to invest in high-tax countries.

There have been numerous proposals to "fix the tax code" internationally. One proposal that would provide for a country-neutral tax system would be for all countries to tax businesses at the same rate (so that a country's corporate taxes would provide neither an incentive nor a disincentive to invest or manufacture there) and for the United States to retain its foreign tax credit. Governments, however, seem reluctant to cede the ability to change tax policy and appear to be less willing to equalize taxes than, for example, to equalize import tariff rates under a free trade or other agreement. A proposal that would favor keeping investment and production in the United States would be to retain the system of worldwide taxation for U.S. companies but to impose higher taxes on investments or income derived from abroad. One proposal to accomplish this would be to permit only a deduction from income, and not a credit to be deducted from the total tax bill, for taxes paid abroad. Other proposals are to end provisions that allow companies to defer foreign-source income indefinitely, to restrict deductions for costs associated with deferred income, or to neutralize the tax benefits for companies moving their "headquarters" to a tax haven (such as Bermuda or the Cayman Islands). Another proposal, however, that would respond to the globalization of businesses is to exempt U.S. companies from paying taxes on their overseas income from investments.[27]

Numerous other tax provisions affect U.S. businesses and their manufacturing decisions. The taxation of income by Americans working abroad, the rate of taxation of corporations, various tax incentives or rebates aimed at promoting specific desired activities (such as technological change), the taxation of corporate dividends, and other tax-related issues are being debated widely. These are beyond the purview of this report.

As with other policies and their impact on global supply networks, the issue is twofold. Is the predominant effect of a change in policy one of diversion or creation? Does a change divert production from the U.S. economy to a foreign location, or does it draw production toward a U.S.-based location? Does the change create more production overall, or does it discourage economic activity?

Trade and investment policy

Global supply trains could not exist without international trade. Traditionally, trade and investment policy deals with border barriers. These include customs duties, import quotas, the freedom to move capital across borders, and the right to establish businesses (including taking over an existing company) in a given country. The development of globalized supply networks does not alter the role of traditional trade and investment policies.

Tariffs or customs duties are national taxes imposed on imports (and sometimes exports) and were originally used primarily to raise revenues for governments, particularly those with weak systems for collecting taxes. Currently for most industrialized countries, the main purposes of tariffs and quotas are to provide protection for domestic industries, to offset some of the cost advantage of foreign suppliers, and also to generate income for governments.

For the major countries of the world, average tariff rates are now quite low (2.9% for the 10 advanced industrialized nations) but higher at 9.8% for the 142 developing nations of the world.[28]

In the United States, certain import-sensitive products may have relatively high tariff rates (e.g., 25% for pickup trucks, 50% for cotton jackets/coats). Other nations also protect certain sectors either through high tariffs or stringent import quotas.

With respect to supply chains, border barriers still raise the cost of imports regardless of whether the product is traded within a supply chain or is traded in open markets. An established supply chain, however, is likely to be less sensitive to border barriers, since such networks are based on long-term relationships and established lines of communication. Over the long-term, however, if border barriers are raised or lowered enough to offset other non-monetary considerations, companies may change the location of manufacturing or other segment of the manufacturing process. Border barriers play a greater role in business decisions on initial plant location, but such decisions also call into play the whole range of factors affecting the competitiveness of the location being considered. Traditional trade and investment policy, therefore, still appears viable in pursuing U.S. goals of economic growth, employment, and a rising standard of living over the long term.

Currently, three major avenues exist to reduce tariffs. First, tariff reductions and other trade liberalizing measures are being negotiated on a multilateral basis through the World Trade Organization (WTO), although the current Doha Round is stalled.[29] Second, on a bilateral or regional basis, countries are negotiating free or preferential trade agreements.[30] Countries also provide trade preferences to certain nations (particularly those with the lowest income levels) or nations with special historical relationships (e.g., former member of an empire). A third, but rarely used method, is to provide normal trade relations status (most favored nation status) to a country that currently does not enjoy such status (e.g., North Korea, Cuba).

Two major avenues are used to increase tariffs or other barriers to trade. For countries that are members of the WTO, tariffs are bound (normally cannot be increased), but they can be raised as a result of various escape clause or market disruption cases. The escape clause or safeguard procedures include anti-dumping or countervailing duty investigations. Also current U.S. tariffs as actually applied tend to be lower than the levels that are bound under World Trade Organization agreements. A second method is through trade sanctions imposed for security or other political considerations (e.g., banning trade with Burma/Myanmar).[31] The use of dispute settlement mechanisms (at the World Trade Organization or provided for in free trade agreements), the use of escape clauses, and invoking safeguard procedures provide a way to target trade policy at a specific product.

A complication in trade policy caused by the globalization of supply networks occurs in the incidence of policy. An increase in customs duties in the United States, for instance, may end up raising costs not only for the foreign exporter but for the American headquarters of a company that has a supply chain with a foreign subsidiary that manufactures the product for export to the United States. It also usually raises the cost of the import to the American consumer.

For example, some have proposed raising tariffs on all imports from China in response to its arguably undervalued exchange rate, a rate which is seen as making Chinese exports cheaper and harming import-competing industries in the United States. Under traditional economic models, imposing tariffs on imports from China would increase the price of such imports (assuming no change in exchange rates), reduce the quantity of imports from China purchased in the United States, and shift some production either to a competing supplier located in the United States or to an exporter in another country that makes similar products. Such protection of domestic industries helps import-competing industries in the United States and hurts exporters from China, although it also may help exporters from Mexico, Southeast Asia, or other countries that make products that compete with those from China. However, more than half of China's exports originate from foreign-owned or foreign-affiliated companies located there. Most of these companies are parts of globalized supply networks. A Chinese exporter, therefore, actually may be a company wholly or partly owned by an American multinational corporation. An increase in an import tariff, therefore, may help U.S. companies competing with imports from China, but it also may end up hurting the U.S. headquarter company as well as its associated Chinese supplier. It also may hurt a U.S. retail-oriented supply chain (such as a discount big box store) that stocks its shelves with items from China.

Debate over the Korea-U.S. Free Trade Agreement (KORUS FTA) also highlighted the effect of globalized supply networks on trade policy. Among the Big Three U.S. automakers, Ford and Chrysler were reported as opposing the KORUS FTA, while GM has remained neutral. GM's position is thought to stem partly from its ownership of Daewoo Motors in Korea.[32] Opponents of the FTA point out that the United States exported only 6,500 cars to Korea in 2007 (for a market share of less than 5%), while Korean automakers sold 775,000 automobiles in the United States (for a market share of nearly 3 0%). What these figures do not indicate, however, is that GM Daewoo sold some 125,000 automobiles in the Korean market in 2007. If these cars are counted as U.S. sales there, the American market share in Korea would be about 12.8%. That is still considerably less than the 30% market share for Korean automakers in the U.S. market, but this Korean share also includes about 250,000 vehicles that were made at the Hyundai plant in Alabama.[33] This illustrates the complexity for policy caused by multinational corporations with significant operations in foreign countries. In the GM case, its Korean operations are primarily aimed at the Korean market, and Hyundai's U.S. operations are mainly aimed at the U.S. market. Each subsidiary hires local workers, while profits (not reinvested) flow back to the parent companies.

Countries around the world currently are actively engaged in negotiating bilateral and regional free-trade agreements (FTA). FTAs normally contain provisions that require a phased reduction or elimination of tariffs by each side and either elimination or expansion of import quotas. FTAs also address a range of other trade-related issues, such as investment flows, access for service providers, and protection of intellectual property rights. The United States already has FTAs with fourteen countries: Canada and Mexico (NAFTA), Israel, Jordan, Morocco, Singapore, Chile, Bahrain, and certain Central American nations (CAFTA). FTAs with Columbia, Panama, and South Korea have been negotiated but await congressional approval, and several more are in the process of being negotiated.

What effect does an FTA have on a global supply chain? For the sake of brevity, consider a reduction in tariffs under an FTA between the United States and another country such as Thailand. The United States and Thailand have had intermittent talks on establishing a U.S.-Thailand FTA. The United States has an average tariff rate of 2.7% while Thailand's is 10%. Eliminating import duties in the United States on products from Thailand implies that the assembled price of the product imported into the U.S. market avoids an increase in cost that would have been collected by U.S. Customs at the port of entry. Depending on the number of competing products in the domestic market, such tariff costs usually are passed on to the consumer or absorbed by the producer. Eliminating the tariff, therefore, either reduces costs to the U.S. consumer or increases profitability of the import supply chain. It also decreases U.S. government revenues and increases the incentive to produce in Thailand. This may divert production from the U.S. market, even though certain parts of the supply chain still located in the United States may become more profitable and employ more workers (e.g., research and development, branding, advertising, and management).

Eliminating import duties in Thailand have a comparable effect on U.S. exports there. The cost of U.S. products in Thailand would be reduced for the Thai consumer, and U.S. exports would be expected to increase. The impact of the mutual tariff reductions on the U.S. balance of trade with Thailand depends on how responsive imports in each country are to tariff reductions (demand elasticities) and the size of the trade flows before the FTA is implemented.

In addition to the bilateral trade effects, FTAs also may affect trade with other countries through the diversion of product flows. The increased trade or production within the FTA countries may either be a net addition to economic activity in the countries involved (because of the larger bilateral market) or a diversion of economic activity away from other countries and into the countries in question. In most cases, countries that negotiate FTAs with the United States also participate in other bilateral and regional FTAs. For example, Thailand also has an FTA-type agreement with China. The combination of the two FTAs would provide a two-fold incentive for the U.S. producer. If the U.S. company has assembly operations in Thailand but obtains parts or components from the United States or from China (with whom it also as an FTA), the U.S. company may ship more parts and components directly from the United States and China to Thailand and bring more finished product to the American and other markets. If the U.S. company provides raw materials for parts or components shipped to Thailand from either the United States or China, U.S. exports would tend to rise but to do so less than if the final product were manufactured directly in the United States and then shipped to Thailand. Either way, the income earned by the U.S. company managing the supply chain would tend to rise. Any increase in profits to the U.S. company could be repatriated to the United States or could be reinvested abroad.[34]

The net effect on a supply chain and the U.S. trade balance because of a cut in tariffs under an FTA, therefore, depends on the relative magnitude of the tariff reductions on each side, the nature of and location of the supply chain, and the responsiveness of trade flows to tariff reductions. In general, however, since U.S. tariffs tend to be lower than those of FTA partner countries, the greater benefit of trade liberalization arguably will go to U.S.-based companies.

For an American company with a global production network, the more countries that participate in a free trade area the better. Such a "common market" with no internal tariffs not only eliminates the need to pay duties as components and final products circulate within the national borders defining the FTA, but it also reduces the required documentation and calculations to determine country of origin. U.S. multinational companies generally support efforts to establish regional free trade areas and to eliminate border barriers.[35]

The growing maze of bilateral FTAs, however, pose a different problem for businesses, particularly for their operations in other countries. For example, Thailand has become a manufacturing location for many companies. Thailand has had held talks with the United States on establishing a bilateral FTA, has signed a limited FTA with China, has a framework agreement with India, and has broad FTAs with Australia and New Zealand and with other members of the Association of Southeast Asian Nations. It also is in FTA discussions with Japan, India, and Peru. If each FTA that has been implemented has different provisions and rules, the cost of complying with rules of origin requirements or the paperwork involved in documenting that the goods fall under the FTA may exceed the lower tariffs provided by the FTA. Some international businesses have indicated that because of the "nuisance" cost of complying with rules of origin or other requirements in FTAs, they just pay the usual tariff rather than try to qualify for a lower FTA rate.[36] This is an argument for the U.S. approach of using a "template" for FTAs in order to ensure consistency across such agreements.

Other aspects of international trade and investment policy include the right of establishment of foreign-owned businesses in countries and the right to national treatment. In essence, these rights ensure that foreign-owned and domestic companies are treated equally both in terms of the right to establish and operate a business and in terms of applicable laws and government action. National treatment also may allow governments to prohibit foreign companies from doing anything not allowed for domestic companies. With the exception of foreign investment that raises security or antitrust complications,[37] the United States provides both national rights of establishment and national treatment as do the countries that are members of the WTO. The more established these rights are in countries, the more likely that globalized supply networks will consider locating in those countries—including in the United States.

How successful is the United States in attracting segments of global supply chains? Data on investments by U.S. and foreign multinational corporations indicate that the United States has been an attractive market for foreign direct investments (FDI, investments in a controlling interest [at least 10% of equity] in productive assets by a foreign corporation). In 2007, FDI in the United States was $232.8 billion of which $144.9 billion (62%) came from Europe. Of the total, $108.1 billion (46%) was in manufacturing.[38] On balance, however, U.S. corporations invest more abroad in productive assets than foreigners invest in the United States. In 2007, U.S. direct investment abroad was $313.8 billion with $55.2 billion (18%) invested in foreign manufacturing.[39]

Labor and health care costs

Labor costs

Labor costs are one of the most controversial aspects of globalized manufacturing chains .[40] The argument is that U.S. companies are "shipping jobs overseas" or "outsourcing jobs" in search of cheap labor to reduce costs of production.[41] In 2006, for example, hourly compensation costs for production workers were $23.82 in the United States, $25.74 in Canada, $3.72 in Mexico, $14.72 in Korea, $34.21 in Germany, and an estimated $0.67 in China.[42]

One of the major drivers of globalized manufacturing networks has been to internalize differences in labor costs within the supply chain. Companies match wages, productivity, and skills with the variety of tasks required in the production process. Tasks requiring skilled workers, such as design, engineering, research and development, and marketing, tend to be located in high wage areas (such as the United States, Europe, Japan, and Singapore), while those requiring low skilled workers, such as assembly and packaging, tend to be located in low wage areas. Companies that produce in the United States also must do such skill and wage matching (such as Caterpillar or Boeing) by locating assembly or supplying plants in lower cost regions and by establishing global supply chains to import certain parts or materials from lower cost countries in Asia, Latin America, and elsewhere. In most cases, companies with assembly plants in the United States buy some manufacturing inputs from abroad.

It also should be noted that firms tend to cluster to take advantage of concentrations of skills, similar production processes, and specialized suppliers. Within the United States, there is Silicon Valley in California, the Research Triangle, in North Carolina, the High-Tech Community along Route 128 in Boston, financial services and transportation in Atlanta, and plastics and aerospace in Wichita, Kansas. The same is true for clusters of industries abroad, including financial services in London, medical research and development in Singapore, and fashion design in Paris. These centers seem to attract industries regardless of their relatively high cost of labor. Studies of such clusters indicate that the most important sources of prosperity can be created and are not dependent on "inherited" advantages, such as relative wage costs.[43]

Still, the difference in labor costs between, for example, the United States and China ($23.82 per hour vs $0.67 in 2006) are striking. The level of wages, however, is not the only factor in determining where segments of the supply chain are located. Labor costs, for many products, account for a relatively small share of total manufacturing costs, and high wages can be offset by high productivity. However, the fracturing of the production process implies that the labor- intensive segment of a supply chain can be concentrated in a low-wage country. For example, fashion design may be centered in Paris, but garment assembly still may be done in lower wage locations.

Low wages, though, may not stay low. American businesses in China, for example, have found that once workers gain certain skills, there is so much competition for those workers that their wages are bid up by competitor companies. Also inflation rates, exchange rate appreciation, and rising shipping costs can offset some of the wage differential. When this is combined with political risk, product safety concerns, and other factors, the supply chain manager may not always choose the country with the lowest wages. For example, wages in Bangladesh may be even lower than those in China, but for a variety of reasons (e.g., low labor productivity, lack of supporting infrastructure, and shipping costs), Bangladesh has not become a major manufacturing platform for U.S. businesses.

A 2007 survey of U.S. companies in China indicated that a major shift in perceptions is occurring regarding China as a low-cost country. Companies there have been experiencing increases of 7% to 10% per year in costs for white collar management, support staff, blue-collar workers, and raw materials. More than half of the companies surveyed agreed or strongly agreed that India, Thailand, and Vietnam are challenging China's position as the leading low-cost export platform. In the survey, the leading reason for establishing manufacturing bases in China was access to the local market with labor costs savings second and access to the Asian market third.[44]

Those who oppose moving segments of supply chains from the United States to foreign countries where labor costs are lower generally raise issues such as lower labor standards and working conditions abroad.[45] In cases, they have put pressure on the U.S. headquarters of the supply chain to require higher labor standards from its supplier companies located in countries such as China. Some large U.S. companies have adopted workplace codes of conduct for their Chinese suppliers.[46]

Labor standards have become an issue in various free trade agreements negotiated by the United States. In a May 2007 "Bipartisan Agreement on Trade Policy" the Bush Administration and leaders of Congress agreed to include certain provisions related to labor (as well as the environment and intellectual property rights) in trade agreements.[47]

An early implementation of this trade deal appeared in the pending free trade agreement with Peru. On June 25, 2007, the United States and Peru signed amendments to the pending U.S.-Peru Trade Promotion Agreement that included labor provisions from the bipartisan trade deal. This included a statement that the United States and Peru would be required to adopt, maintain and enforce their own labor laws as well as five basic internationally-recognized labor standards, as stated in the 1998 International Labor Organization Declaration. These included (1) freedom of association; (2) the effective recognition of the right to collective bargaining; (3) the elimination of all forms of forced or compulsory labor; (4) the effective abolition of child labor and a prohibition on the worst forms of child labor; and (5) the elimination of discrimination in respect of employment and occupation. The Peru amendments also provide that any decision made by a signatory on the distribution of enforcement resources would not be a reason for not complying with the labor provisions, and that parties would not be allowed to derogate from labor obligations in a manner affecting trade or investment.[48]

Labor issues also have been raised in debates over proposed free trade agreements with Columbia, Panama, and South Korea as well as in considering renewal of trade promotion authority.[49]

The declining share of U.S. employment accounted for by manufacturing over the past half century has long been a concern for policymakers. For the 21 sub-sectors comprising the manufacturing sector in the United States, between the fourth quarter of 2000 and third quarter of 2008, employment declined by 22% or 3.8 million jobs. This occurred despite an increase of 7 million jobs in all private employment—excluding manufacturing.[50] The decline in employment can be traced to increases in labor productivity and import competition but also is related to the focus on core competencies in global supply chains and the outsourcing of noncore functions (such as accounting, security, shipping, and janitorial services provided by companies in the service sector). Increases in productivity and technological change are part of the normal development of an economy. Most workers displaced by technology find employment elsewhere, although some may be negatively affected (lower wages, fewer benefits) for some period of time.

Those displaced by imports, however, may find it difficult to transfer their skills to other industries because they tend to be in traditional industries, such as apparel, leather, textile mills, and primary metals.[51] In apparel, for example, the global supply chains include producers (such as brand name clothing manufacturers) who may contract with overseas suppliers to manufacture garments according to their specifications with their brand labels. Apparel supply chains also include big box retailers who may source and sell product both from U.S. brand name suppliers and from non-U.S. manufacturers located in markets around the world. While the lower prices enabled by the various supply chains may benefit the consumer, and the wholesale and retail sectors in the United States claim much of the revenue from sales of the imported product, the import-competing industries may turn to the government for help through programs such as Trade Adjustment Assistance in retaining workers[52] or for assistance in retooling factories or in pursuing innovations or through trade remedy laws.

Health care costs

In the United States, much of health care is provided by employers, so health care costs have become an integral part of labor costs. The costs for health care in the United States are the highest in the world. The Congressional Budget Office (CBO) estimates that spending on health care and related activities will account for about 17% of gross domestic product in 2009 ($2.6 trillion or $8,300 per capita) and under current law CBO projected that share to reach nearly 20% ($13,000 per capita) by 2017.[53]

Business interests have claimed that these costs are hurting the ability of U.S.-based businesses to compete in world markets and are causing firms to move production to other countries.[54] General Motors, for example cites health care costs as a major burden when compared with manufacturers in Japan and Europe.[55] This issue is complex, and reform to improve the competitiveness of the U.S. market as a base for supply chain operations is but one consideration in a range of factors pushing health care reform high onto the agenda of many interest groups. Organizations representing international business agree that something needs to be done to reduce the cost of health care paid by businesses, but there is less of a consensus on the specifics of how that could be achieved.[56]

Environmental regulation

As with labor issues, environmental regulation both as applied to businesses in the United States and as contained in various international trade and other agreements tends to be quite controversial. The issue for governments is how to find a balance between three potentially conflicting objectives: security of supply, industrial competitiveness, and environmental sustainability.[57]

For the U.S.-based part of global supply chains, environmental regulation may affect costs of production[58] as well as consumer perceptions and demand. Foes of globalization and international supply chains, moreover, sometimes accuse U.S. businesses of sourcing products overseas where environmental requirements may be less stringent and compliance less costly. One solution proposed is to harmonize environmental regulations across countries.

The May 2007 "Bipartisan Agreement on Trade Policy" between Congressional leaders and the Bush Administration contained key provisions related to the environment. In the agreement, the Administration and Congress agreed to incorporate a specific list of multilateral environmental agreements in free trade agreements. The list included the Convention on International Trade in Endangered Species, Montreal Protocol on Ozone Depleting Substances, Convention on Marine Pollution, Inter-American Tropical Tuna Convention, Ramsar Convention on Wetlands, International Whaling Convention, and Convention on Conservation of Antarctic Marine Living Resources.

The competitiveness of U.S. industry often is raised in debates over environmental policy. The policy discussion on greenhouse gasses, for example, turned partly on the effect of environmental policy on the ability of companies to compete in the global marketplace. If a country has legally binding carbon control restrictions while others do not, the potential exists that the country with the restrictions will find itself at a competitive disadvantage vis-à-vis countries without comparable policies and could lose global market share for certain carbon emitting production. In addition, this potential shift in production could result in some of the U.S. carbon reductions being counteracted by increased production in less regulated countries (commonly known as "carbon leakage").[59] Debates over environmental policy, therefore, often center on what can be categorized as the three-Cs: Cost, Competitiveness, and Comprehensiveness.[60]

Supply chains also have entered into policy debates over other environmental issues, such as illegal logging and sustainable development. Some headquarters firms have been targeted for protest because of actions of overseas members of their supply chains.

Currencies and exchange rates

Exchange rates determine the value of one currency in terms of another. The exchange rates of most industrialized nations are allowed to float while many developing nations actively intervene to manage their exchange rates. For floating currencies, their value is determined by international financial transactions with occasional intervention by governments. Managed exchange rates usually are pegged to or managed against either one currency, such as the dollar, or to a basket of currencies that usually contains the dollar along with currencies such as the Euro or Japanese yen. China has such an exchange rate regime.

Exchange rates can change dramatically over relatively short periods of time relative to the life of a typical manufacturing chain. When the value of the dollar declines, it increases the dollar cost of all products produced in countries whose currency has appreciated relative to the dollar. If a country's exchange rate is tied to the value of the dollar, that currency will decline in tandem with dollar, and the dollar depreciation will have no effect on the price of goods traded between the two countries. The prices of goods traded with countries without a dollar tie (such as Europe, Japan, India, or South Korea), however, will change. A country that ties the value of its currency to the dollar, however, still has to pursue policies to maintain its exchange rate that may cause domestic interest rates to rise or the rate of inflation to increase.

Figure 6 shows the value of several currencies relative to the dollar since January 2004. This has been a period of high volatility in exchange rates with the Canadian dollar up by 34% at one point in 2005 before dropping to almost parity in December 2008, the Japanese yen down by 12% in 2005 but up 16% at the end of 2008, and the Chinese Renminbi (RMB) up by 21% since Beijing announced its managed float in July 2005. The Euro also has risen and fallen over the period. At the end of 2008, the Korean won was 33% below its peak in October 2007.

The effect of currency appreciation on a supply chain can be illustrated by the Chinese RMB.[61] The appreciation of the RMB has a similar effect on production costs (calculated in U.S. dollars) as a wage (or other cost) increase in China. However, it has one major difference. Exchange rates fluctuate more than wage rates. Exchange rates move in both directions, while wage rates tend to be "sticky downward." They rise but rarely fall. A supply chain manager, therefore, is less likely to shift production because of an appreciation in China's exchange rate than in response to a comparable rise in wages. In China's case, however, the exchange and wage rates are both moving in the same direction. Together they work to magnify the increase in costs to manufacture there.

Over the long term, however, exchange rate appreciation can dramatically affect the relative cost of production in a country. At the time of the Plaza Accord in September 1985, for example, the Japanese yen was worth 230 yen per dollar. At the end of 2008, the rate had been around 90 yen per dollar for a 155% appreciation in the yen. This greatly affected the price competitiveness of products exported from Japan and also many of its imports and has been a major factor in the movement of considerable amounts of production by Japanese multinational companies to locations overseas.

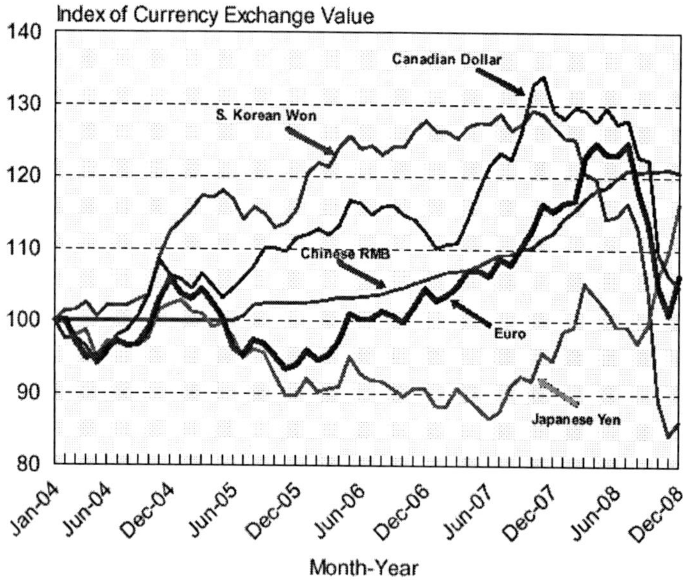

Source: Congressional Research with Data from PACIFIC Exchange Rate Service.

Figure 6. Indexes of Currency Values Relative to the U.S. Dollar for the Canadian Dollar, S.Korean Won, Chinese RMB, Euro, and Japanese Yen

In a survey of U.S. manufacturers in 2008, 40% of 500 survey participants indicated that the value of the dollar had an effect on where they choose to source their business. At the time of the survey, the value of the dollar was falling, and nearly half of the responses said that they were already sourcing more business in the United States.

Infrastructure and transportation

Global supply chains could not exist without efficient transportation networks supported by infrastructure (ports, roads, railroads, airports, etc.) that enable products within the manufacturing network to move freely from one segment of the chain to the next. Infrastructure also can be defined to include the electrical grid, pipelines, the Internet, or telecommunications equipment. The issue of infrastructure in general is beyond the purview of this report.[62]

One part of infrastructure and transportation that is critical to global supply chains seems to be oceanic shipping and air freight. The oceans are no longer a barrier that isolates and protects countries. Instead, modern communications and transportation have brought markets of the world onto each other's doorsteps. The oceans and skies have become avenues of interaction rather than barriers of separation. Shipping, however, raises certain issues for public policy. These revolve around risks in the supply chain, particularly costs, security risks and delays in shipping.

The spike in petroleum prices in 2007-2008 exposed a vulnerability of oceanic and other transportation to a critical cost variable. When the price of oil rose to $140 per barrel, the cost of shipping a standard 40-foot container from Shanghai to the United States rose to $8,000 compared with $3,000 early in the decade. Shipping speeds also were reduced to conserve on fuel. The increase in shipping costs was equivalent to a 9% import tariff on trade or what amounted to a reversal of most of the trade liberalization that had been accomplished over the previous three decades.[63] the net result of the rise in shipping costs was that some companies switched production to locations closer to home, some in the United States.[64]

For example, in October 2007, the cost of shipping residential heaters from China to Bowling Green, Kentucky became too high for Desa LLC, and the company shifted manufacturing operations back to the United States. Not only had the cost of ocean shipping risen but the 2,000 mile inland trucking costs from the West Coast to Kentucky (along with a cut in the export rebate by the Chinese government, rise in price of Chinese steel, and the rising value of the Chinese currency) also made sourcing from China unprofitable.[65]

About 12 million standardized shipping containers arrive at U.S. seaports annually. With the exception of automobiles or bulk commodities, this the preferred method for transporting manufactured goods from overseas factories to wholesale distributors in the United States. Air freight is more expensive but is critical for lighter products such as electronic components used in "just-in-time" assembly operations. The possibility that a shipping container sent from a foreign port might contain terrorism-related devices, weapons, counterfeit products, and other prohibited items has raised concerns over container security to a new level. A distinct trade-off exists, however, between ensuring security and facilitating the free flow of commerce. For example, the Maritime Commerce Security Plan of the U.S. Department of Homeland Security states that the plan is to improve the security of the maritime supply chain to lower the risk that it will be used to support terrorism while at the same time to protect and facilitate lawful maritime commerce.[66]

Simply stated, the question for policy makers relative to global supply chains and shipping rests on what measures are required to reduce the probability of a terrorist or other incident without unduly interfering with commerce. In the 110th Congress, for example, H.R. 1 (P.L. 110-53), "Implementing Recommendations of the 9/11 Commission Act of 2007" required by the year 2012 container scanning by imaging and radiation detection equipment at a foreign port before a container is loaded. The SAFE Port Act enacted in 2006 required, among other things, that U.S. Customs and Border Protection (CBP) conduct a pilot program to determine the feasibility of scanning 100% of U.S.-bound containers. In order to fulfill this and other requirements, in December 2006, the CBP and the U.S. Department of Energy jointly announced the formation of the Secure Freight Initiative.[67]

Scanning

While the security benefits associated with the requirement for 100% scanning of all cargo containers bound for the United States seem to be obvious and apparent, actual implementation has raised numerous issues. This is one example of the tradeoff between national security and supply chain efficiency.

In testimony before Congress in 2008, the U.S. Government Accountability Office laid out the major challenges related to this requirement. Among them were concerns over the lack of information on the efficacy of host government examination systems, additional time and cost requirements (particularly for equipment placed miles from where the cargo containers are stored and the comparatively short period of time containers are available for scanning when transshipped), the inconsistency with widely accepted risk management principles, and the possibility that foreign governments would call for reciprocity of 100% scanning by the United States of outbound containers.[68]

Many foreign shippers, port authorities, and U.S. businesses overseas are viewing this goal of 100% scanning with some alarm.[69] Shanghai, for example, is the world's second most busy port with total container throughput of 26.1 million units in 2007.[70] In Shanghai most containers are shipped from manufacturers on smaller boats that gather at an island port offshore where they are loaded onto ocean going vessels. Scanning a container as it is being transferred from one boat to another is extremely difficult.[71] The American Chamber of Commerce in China has stated that, the scanning of every container bound for the United States "will no doubt lead to major logistics bottlenecks as the massive volume of shipped goods funnels through a limited number of scanning stations. This is a potential deal-breaker for perishable goods and just-in-time supply."[72]

Singapore has the world's largest container shipping center. Singapore is the 13th largest source of U.S. imports and accounted for 13% of all U.S. imports of goods in 2007. Singapore's Ports Command of the Immigration and Checkpoints Authority reported that in 2007 it was scanning about 15% of the 24 million cargo containers that pass through its ports each year. It is able to scan an incoming container truck in a few minutes, although the scan takes extra time to set up and interpret the results. Singapore signed on early to the Cargo Security Initiative of the United States and has been operating for several years as a pilot port. The Authority indicated its concern that the American side keeps announcing new initiatives (e.g., the Megaports Initiative and the Secure Freight Initiative) that seem to overlap and have different sponsoring agencies. With so many containers being handled, the port authority also is concerned that even adding a few seconds to the handling of each container would have cumulative effects on the efficiency of its operations. It views with dread the requirement for 100% container screening.[73]

In April 2008, the Association of German Seaport Operators (Zentralverband der Deutschen Seehafenbetriebe, ZDS) sharply critiqued the 100% scanning requirement. ZDS argued that scanning 100% of United States bound container cargo would require tremendous financial outlays and time. The port of Hamburg, for example, ships 120,000 containers to the United States per year. At a cost of 300 ($375) per container, additional outlays would reach 36 million ($45 million) per year not counting the 15 minutes per container for an assessment (and longer for the containers tagged for physical inspection).[74] On the airfreight side, however, in October 2008, the United States and the European Union did reach an agreement for screening air cargo on U.S.-bound passenger aircraft.[75]

Logistics security in China

In 2007, the Global Supply Chain Council in Shanghai conducted a survey of international companies there dealing with secure logistics. The respondents indicated that security in logistics had become an important element in their strategy and operations. Many of the companies surveyed had reorganized their international supply chains to comply with new international regulations, such as the Container Security Initiative. In addition, many technological initiatives had been launched that were aimed at improving the security of the supply chain. These included the use of radio frequency identification, E-seals (physical locking mechanisms with technology to detect and report tampering), satellite supported tracking of containers, electronic locks, image recognition devices, and biometric identification.

In this survey, 62% indicated that security was a critical factor for their company. The respondents considered the probability of a terrorist attack low. They were more concerned with damage due to neglect by their own employees or theft. They were the least concerned with smuggling of cargo or people. Two thirds of the respondents in the survey had been engaged in working with and certifying known suppliers and service providers, introducing security and audit procedures, using information technology for more visibility, and using dual sourcing. The number of companies that had audited their own procedures was twice as high as the number of companies that had audited their partners in their supply chain.

Product and food safety

The safety of imported manufactured products and food gained significant attention in 2007 when items such as lead in paint, adulterated pet food, and melamine in milk products, drew wide public attention.[76] Fears of mad cow disease also have hurt U.S. beef exports.[77] Until the recent rise in such cases, companies manufacturing abroad often were less likely to take measures to ensure quality in purchased inputs than they did in their own production processes. Now, however, companies are realizing that their reputation as a company and their whole supply chain can break down if even a single sub-contractor provides a defective product.

In response to cases of tainted imports from China, the United States and China have reached a number of agreements to address health and safety concerns. These agreements were negotiated by U.S. agencies such as the Consumer Product Safety Commission, the National Highway Traffic Safety Administration, and the U.S. Department of Health and Human Services and their counterparts in China.[78]

The U.S. Department of Agriculture through its Food Safety and Inspection Service also has developed guidelines for processors, retailers, wholesalers, and logistics providers involved in meat, poultry, and egg product supply chains.[79] In 2004, the U.S. Department of Homeland Security established the National Center for Food Protection and Defense (NCFPD) at the University of Minnesota. The NCFPD is a multidisciplinary and action-oriented research consortium charged with addressing the vulnerability of the nation's food system to attack through intentional contamination with biological or chemical agents. The program takes a comprehensive, farm-to-table view of the food system and examines all aspects of the system from primary production through transportation and food processing to retail and food service.[80]

Education and training

The ability of American firms to compete in the global marketplace, depends partly on the availability of skilled workers and managers. Also, rapid advances in science and technology are a continual challenge to the scientific and technical proficiency of the U.S. workforce.[81] For policymakers, the issue centers on (1) whether U.S. public education adequately prepares young people for the realities of the marketplace; (2) whether the system prepares enough students to pursue rigorous programs of study in science and technology; (3) whether U.S. education and other institutions promote innovation sufficiently for the United States to remain at the forefront of scientific and technological advances; (4) whether sufficient opportunity is provided for adults to be retrained and retooled; and (5) the extent to which companies may rely on foreign workers for certain jobs.

The analysis of these issues is beyond the purview of this report. Congress has recently addressed some of these issues in the context of the nation's science and technology (S&T) workforce.[82] A premise in promoting a better-trained and equipped S&T workforce is that such workers are essential in generating new ideas and technology that can lead to new business opportunities and jobs for the domestic economy. Another premise is that for high-technology firms to locate operations in the United States, there must be

S&T savvy employees to work in the companies. The 110th Congress passed the America Competes Act (P.L. 110-69) to address concerns regarding the science and technology workforce and education. Other issues considered included demographic trends and the future S&T talent pool, the current S&T workforce and changing workforce needs, and the influence of foreign S&T students and workers on the U.S. S&T workforce.

Protection of intellectual property

An important part of the legal, financial, and economic environment in which a company operates is the protection of intellectual property rights (IPR). Intellectual property includes patents, copyrights, trade secrets, trade marks, and geographical indications (use of a geographical name in branding or promoting a distinctive product, an action designed to take advantage of the quality and reputation of a product originating in a certain region). IPR violations are claimed to cost U.S. manufacturers billions of dollars each year in lost sales. There is also concern about the potential health and safety consequences of counterfeit pharmaceutical drugs and other products, as well as the link between terrorist groups and organized crime and traffic in counterfeit and pirated goods.[83]

In the 110th Congress, legislation (P.L. 110-403) was enacted to establish a new structure to coordinate federal IPR enforcement activities. The role of Congress in addressing IPR and trade- related issues stems from the power to regulate international trade in the U.S. Constitution. Section 337 of the Tariff Act of 1930 (19 U.S.C. 1337) is the primary option available to U.S. companies to protect themselves from imports into the United States of goods made by foreign companies that infringe U.S. intellectual property rights. The U.S. International Trade Commission (ITC) administers Section 337 investigations. Since 2001, over 90% of unfair competition acts asserted under Section 337 have involved patent infringement.[84]

Global supply chains enable product makers to exert considerably more control over their property rights in companies abroad who are part of their production process when compared with those producers who procure parts or products from completely unrelated suppliers. Still companies face cases of technology leakage, reverse engineering, and counterfeiting of products by parties whether located in domestic or in foreign markets. They also create sensitive strategic issues about technology transfer or how much intellectual property or defense-related technology embedded in equipment can be made available to supply chain partners overseas.[85]

Global supply chains can, however, provide a presence in the foreign market for the company with claim to intellectual property at risk. This may provide a segue into the foreign government policymaking structure through the U.S. company with standing there. When a U.S. company is incorporated abroad, it can become a "naturalized" actor in the political process there. Appeals for stricter enforcement of intellectual property by a locally incorporated company often can complement country-to-country negotiations on IPR issues.

Problems with IPR protection can be found in many countries of the world, including the United States, but are quite common in China. As China has developed, it has become a focus of U.S. efforts to reduce violations of IPR held by American companies. The Chinese government has undertaken anti-piracy campaigns and there is an increasing number of IPR cases in Chinese courts, but overall piracy and counterfeiting levels there still remained high in 2007. U.S. copyright industries estimate that 80% to 95% of all of their members' copyrighted works sold in China were pirated.[86]

Chinese counterfeits include many products, such as pharmaceuticals, electronics, batteries, auto parts, industrial equipment, toys, and many other products, that may be exported and could pose a direct threat to the health and safety of consumers in the United States. Inadequate IPR enforcement is a key factor contributing to these shortcomings. China has high criminal thresholds for prosecution of IPR violations as well as difficulties in initiating cases. This arguably results in limited deterrence. Civil damages are also low.[87]

Free trade agreements negotiated by the United States generally have included chapters that contain provisions that strengthen protection for copyrights, patents, and trademarks, as well as rules for enforcement. Recent free trade agreements, including those with Central American countries, Bahrain, Oman, and Peru have resulted in commitments to strengthen IPR protection and enforcement in those countries. The signed (but not yet approved by Congress) agreements with South Korea, Columbia, and Panama also contain IPR provisions. A number of trade and investment framework agreements with countries also have provisions to enhance intellectual property protection and enforcement.

Risks

In addition to the security, safety, integrity, and currency risks faced by companies with globalized supply chains, a policy risk also exists. A policy risk is the chance that either the home government or a foreign country will enact a change in policy that harms the business operation. U.S. embassies and organizations of U.S. businesses overseas devote considerable effort toward monitoring policy developments of local governments in order to head off adverse policy decisions. These include local content and labor requirements, import and export regulations, and safety provisions. Such policies, frequently pursued for protectionist purposes, often dictate the location of specific global supply chain activities and increase the difficulty of standardizing global supply chain efforts across multiple markets.[88]

In a sense, however, global supply chains may have contributed to political stability among countries. They have created interdependencies among nations that provide incentives for governments to maintain stability in international relationships. This has lessened the prospect of political risk arising from international disputes. The growing economic interdependence between Japan and China, for example, is considered to have had a calming effect on relations when disputes have arisen over history and politics. Taiwanese businesses on the mainland also have pressed their government to relax restrictions on Chinese investment in Taiwan and for more direct airline flights between China and Taiwan.[89] China's trade and investment relations with Southeast Asian nations has had a similar effect in reducing political tensions and in seeking peaceful solutions to thorny issues such as territorial claims. U.S.-China economic interaction likewise seems to have contributed to calmer political and security relations.

For some risks, such as political upheavals, insurance is available to U.S. businesses.[90] Still, political unrest in countries can severely disrupt supply chain operations. Recent political turmoil and street demonstrations in Thailand, for example, have caused multinational companies to exercise more caution in investing there.

As the global financial crisis has demonstrated, multinational firms, particularly in the financial sector may generate risks that domestic regulators either do not recognize or do not address. AIG, the insurance company rescued by the United States in 2008 was brought down primarily by its financial-products unit that marketed credit default swaps. This unit was headquartered in London, not in the United States, and government regulation of such products essentially did not exist.[91] The need for the U.S. government rescue of AIG proved to be a key factor in the spread of what eventually became a global financial crisis and recession.

Fiscal, monetary, and industrial policies

In the current financial crisis, countries around the world are either contemplating or implementing various stimulus packages to help their economies recover from the global slowdown. One way that supply chains enter the debate is in estimating the impact of fiscal policies—particularly government spending or subsidies—on the domestic economy. If, for example, government policy is to inject funds into the economy, where should they be injected in order to maximize the economic (not political) impact of the policy?

Each dollar injected into an economy has what economists call a multiplier effect. This is a rule of thumb that estimates what the final impact of that dollar would be on the total economy after it goes through various rounds of spending. Estimates of the fiscal multiplier vary, but they usually range from about 2 to 4. At the 4-level, each dollar injected into the economy ends up being spent and respent an average of 4 times. The reason the multiplier is not larger is that at each round of spending there is "leakage" from the system. If for example, $1 is given in the form of a tax rebate, the recipient may spend three-fourths of that amount (75¢ in the first round of spending) and may save or is taxed one-fourth of the amount (25¢), by the time all rounds of spending are complete, the eventual effect will be approximately a $4 increase in total spending. As a general rule, therefore, the multiplier effect will be larger the lower the saving and tax rates. These tend to occur in lower income households who tend to save less and are in lower tax brackets. However, lower income households also may purchase more imported goods (lower priced items), so the greater spending by households in the first round may be offset by more leakage because of purchases of imports.

If the funds are provided to a business in the form of a loan or subsidy, the business may spend all of it, but the business may purchase some of its products from abroad or invest the funds in overseas operations. Such spending abroad also constitutes a "leakage" from the domestic economy (in the first round). A question for policy, therefore, is which industries in the United States tend to have the least leakage from imports? In industries with Buy American provisions (such as certain rapid transportation, domestic ship transport, and national defense), leakage is kept small by law. Much government procurement falls under Buy American constraints,[92] although signatory countries to the WTO Government Procurement Agreement must implement requirements to buy local according provisions of the agreement.[93]

Figure 7 shows exports and imports by U.S. multinational companies in selected sectors in 2005. The sectors are ranked according to those with the largest net exports at the top and those with the largest net imports at the bottom.[94] There were many other sectors with data collected by the U.S. Bureau of Economic Analysis in which multinational companies operated, but those sectors had fewer than three companies reporting, and their data was suppressed to avoid disclosure of amounts for individual companies. The rank order in the figure roughly parallels the rank order for size of the fiscal multipliers for the sectors indicated. Food, computers and electronics, machinery, chemicals, metals, and mining tend to have the higher first round effects (less import leakage and more exports), while motor vehicles, retail and wholesale trade, and petroleum products tend to have lower first-round effects (more leakage abroad).

Supply chains have an additional effect that is related to the macroeconomy. If an economy drops into recession or a business contacts, some of the layoffs in a supply chain can occur overseas. Adjusting production by slowing imports has less impact on the U.S. labor force than laying off workers in the United States. The supply chain linkages, however, also imply that a recession in a country as large as the United States may also cause a slowdown in economic activity elsewhere. This coupling of economies in the global marketplace may contribute to the synchronization of recessionary economic conditions and make global recovery even more difficult.

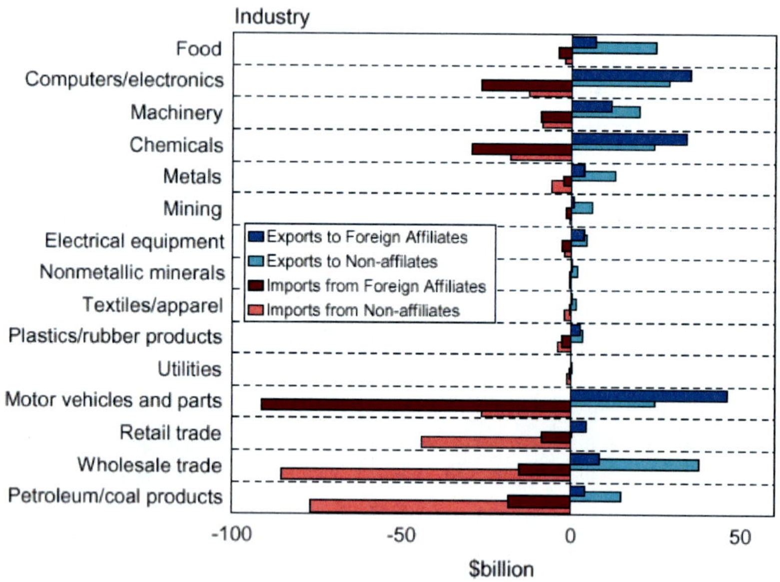

Source: Congressional Research Service with data from U.S.Bureau of Economic Analysis.

Figure 7. Exports and Imports by U.S.Multinational Companies in Selected Industries, 2005

At the microeconomic level, as indicated in the policy discussion above, the impact of policy depends partly on the nature of the policy, itself, but it also depends on how and where along a supply chain the policy is applied. In a typical supply chain, policy points arise all along the process from initial research, branding and design to parts procurement, assembly, packaging, shipping and to final sale. The question is whether specific governmental actions intended to accomplish one goal, actually are able to accomplish that goal given the globalized nature of the industry and profit maximizing behavior of businesses.

Policy Review Mechanisms

In the United States, there are mechanisms in place to review the effect of proposed regulations on U.S. businesses and their ability to compete in the global marketplace. The overall responsibility in the Administration for such review lies with the Office of Management and Budget,[95] but most of the formal analysis of the policies that affect trade and competitiveness are done in the Department of Commerce in the Office of Competition and Economic Analysis. This office provides information on the impact of economic and regulatory policies on the competitiveness of U.S. manufacturing and services industries. It does this by analyzing the effects of both domestic and foreign policy developments on U.S. industries.[96]

The U.S. International Trade Commission (USITC) conducts economic analysis at the request of the Congress and President as well as the Commission itself. The Commission's analysis is used to contribute to the development of sound and informed U.S. international trade policy and to the public debate on issues relating to U.S. international trade and competitiveness. USITC analysis attempts to integrate industry, trade and tariff data with industrial and economic expertise to prepare a wide range of official Commission reports and staff developed articles. The USITC conducts analysis of major international trade proposals including all proposed Free Trade Agreements.[97]

P.L. 110-69 (Sec. 1006) directed the President to establish a President's Council on Innovation and Competitiveness. This Council is to undertake various activities for promoting innovation and competitiveness in the United States, measure progress in such promotion, and report annually to the President and Congress on such progress.

Currently, the U.S. Congress does not have established procedures to evaluate the impact on business supply chains and industrial competitiveness of proposed legislation, although business- related interest groups certainly make their positions known. Within the Congress, the Economic Competitive Caucus (Representative Todd Tiahrt Chairman) focuses on eight areas where it feels the federal government could remove barriers to economic competitiveness for U.S. businesses.

The Congressional Budget Office (CBO) conducts budgetary impact analysis for proposed legislation and analyzes specific policy and program issues related to the budget. The agency undertakes such studies at the request of the Congress. CBO analysis does not usually address, however, the effect of proposed legislation on the competitiveness of U.S. based businesses.[98]

In the U.S. private sector, the Council on Competitiveness is a group of corporate CEOs, university presidents,and labor leaders.It states that its members are committed to enhanced U.S.competitiveness in the global economy through the creation of high-value economic activity in the United States. As a nonpartisan, nongovernmental organization in Washington, D.C., the Council attempts to shape the debate on competitiveness by bringing together business, labor, academic and government leaders to evaluate economic challenges and opportunities.[99]

Much of business input into the impact of U.S. policy on business interests seems to be done through trade associations, labor unions, special interest groups, and various lobbying efforts. The administration also has formal private sector advisory committees, particularly for international trade policy. The United States Trade Representative, for example, has advisory committees dealing with trade policy and negotiations and trade and the environment plus committees representing labor, agriculture, and industry.

In Europe, the European Union requires that all major European Commission initiatives contain an Impact Assessment. Such assessments contain an evaluation of the social, economic, and environmental impacts of various policy options associated with a proposal. The EC encourages estimates to be expressed in qualitative, quantitative, and, where appropriate, monetary terms, although in practice, most assessments are based on surveys of business.[100]

In Sweden, the Board of Swedish Industry and Commerce for Better Regulation (NNR) is an independent, non-partisan organization funded entirely by its members. The membership consists of the 14 largest Swedish business organizations and trade associations with a combined membership of some 300,000 companies. The principal focus of the NNR is regulatory simplification and a more business-friendly environment, not only in Sweden but also in the European Union. One of its principal tasks is to coordinate the business sector's scrutiny of Impact Assessments by the EU and to negotiate with regulatory agencies during the evaluation of the costs and benefits of a new regulation.[101]

CONCLUSION

International business supply chains provide the structure for the new world of globalized business. Much of U.S. international trade is conducted by globalized supply chains. For public policy, supply chains affect the magnitude of impact for fiscal stimulus packages and also the incidence of trade policy. Supply chains also are affected by the range of policies that have an impact on the competitiveness of U.S. business. Whether taxes, environmental regulations, labor policy, or shipping security, business supply chains are directly affected by changes in the business environment, whether in the domestic or foreign markets. In the world of globalized supply chains, a policy aimed at imports, may actually hit U.S. parented supply chains as well as foreign companies and countries.

The fracturing of business into core and non-core competencies and into domestic and foreign segments of supply chains implies that what had been purely domestic economic and regulatory policy now may affect the operations of U.S. parented supply chains abroad, and what had been primarily international economic, trade, and investment policy now also has a clear domestic effect. The globalization of supply has added complexity to both the managers of the supply chains and to policymaking.

As the 111th Congress and the new Administration consider changes to economic policy, the basic issues raised by global supply chains may come into play, particularly considerations of the incidence of policies. For example, is the goal of a policy to support business to promote the overall efficiency and profitability of U.S. parented supply chains even if significant segments of those chains are located abroad, or is the goal to induce companies to move production or other business activity to the United States even if such action reduces supply chain efficiency and the ability of the U.S.-parented supply chain to compete in the global marketplace? In international trade and investment policies, does the incidence of the policy fall on overseas segments of American parented supply chains? If the policy is to reduce imports into the

United States, what effect will that have on global supply chain operations? Is there a balance between trade policies designed to increase U.S. exports (e.g., by reducing tariffs abroad) and those that may induce U.S. companies to move production overseas (e.g., easing foreign country limits on direct investments). As global supply chains attempt to maximize their efficiency and profitability, they face trade-offs between border transaction costs (including tariffs), factor costs (including labor and capital), logistical costs (including shipping), external business costs (ease of doing business, regulations, etc.), and various risks (including security, financial, and political risk). How does government economic policy influence these factors and trade-offs in ways that are in accord with, rather than counter to, U.S. national goals?

End Notes

[1] Globalization refers to the development of an increasingly integrated and interconnected world economy marked by liberalized trade flows, high mobility of capital, transnational businesses, and greater interdependence among national economies.

[2] CRS Report RL34684, *Consumer Product Safety Improvement Act of 2008: P.L. 110-314*, by Margaret Mikyung Lee.

[3] Thomas Anderson, "U.S. Affiliates of Foreign Companies, Operations in 2006," *Survey of Current Business*, August 2008, pp. 186, 196. Raymond J. Mataloni, Jr., "U.S. Multinational Companies, Operations in 2006," *Survey of Current Business*, November 2008, p. 30.

[4] Masao Hisada, "Hitachi's Globalization," a PowerPoint presentation, July 18, 2008.

[5] Crowe Horwath LLP and IW Custom Research, "The Future of Manufacturing," *Industry Week*, November 2008, pp. S3, S4.

[6] Greg Linden, Kenneth L. Kraemer, Jason Dedrick, "Who Captures Value in a Global Innovation System? The Case of Apple's iPod," Personal Computing Industry Center, June 2007. 10 p.

[7] For example, in the third quarter of 2008, GMAC, GM's financing arm, reported a loss of $2.5 billion (of which $294 million was related to auto financing and most of the rest from mortgage financing). In 2006, a consortium of banks and Cerberus Capital Management bought 51% of GMAC from General Motors leaving 49% still in-house. Peter Valdes-Dapena, "GM Dealers Feel Squeeze from GMAC," *CNNMoney.com*, November 6, 2008.

[8] Peter T. Leach, "Weak link: Trade suffers as suppliers struggle to obtain financing," *The Journal of Commerce Online*, December 24, 2008.

[9] The idea of core competencies is that they represent the true sources of competitive advantage and that such competencies should be the focus of firm effort. All other activities could be outsourced. See G. Hamel and C.K. Prahalad. "The Core Competence of the Corporation," *Harvard Business Review*, Vol. 68, No. 3, 1990. Pp. 243-244.

[10] A just-in-time production system is the coordinated manufacture of components or products so that materials are received or produced at the precise time and in the exact quantity to meet the demand of the customer or the next operation in an assembly process. This reduces costs by eliminating the need to hold large inventories of parts and product and allows for defects in parts to be corrected before being incorporated into a product.

[11] See CRS Report RL34001, *U.S. Furniture Manufacturing: Overview and Prospects*, by Stephen Cooney.

[12] L. & J.G. Stickley, Inc., *Our History,* accessed January 7, 2009. *http://www.stickley .com/OurStickleyStory.cfm?SubPgName=OurHistory&BodyTxt=On.*

[13] Larry Rohter, "Shipping costs start to crimp globalization," *International Herald Tribune*, August 2, 2008, Internet version.

[14] The actual quotation in 1953 by Charles Erwin Wilson (former President of General Motors) in his confirmation hearing to become Secretary of Defense was, "For years I thought what was good for our country was good for General Motors, and vice versa."

[15] Adam Smith. *An Inquiry into the Nature and Causes of the Wealth of Nations*. (Dublin, Whitestone, 1776).

[16] Boeing, *787 Dreamliner, Program Fact Sheet*, accessed January 6, 2009. *http://www. boeing.com/commercial/787family/programfacts.html.*

[17] CRS Report 98-568, *Export-Import Bank: Background and Legislative Issues*, by Danielle Langton.

[18] Peter Pae, "Japanese Helping 787 Take Wing," *Los Angeles Times*, May 9, 2005, p. C1.

[19] Reuters, "U.S. to continue challenging Airbus subsidies," *International Herald Tribune*, March 6, 2008.

[20] Jill Jusko, "Reworking the Pharma Supply Chain," *Industry Week*, December 2008, pp. 47-49. Note that in 2008, Pfizer employed about 85,000 people in more than 150 countries. Of its $48.4 billion in revenues in 2007, $8.1 billion was spent on research and development mostly in the United States, the U.K., and in Singapore. See Pfizer, "Pfizer Company Fact Sheet," Updated February 21, 2008; Pfizer Asia Pacific Pte Ltd., "Who We Are;" and Pfizer UK, "Pfizer at a Glance," 2008.

[21] National Association of Manufacturers, "IEAP-01 International Trade Policy

[22] A linear programming is a mathematical method of maximizing or minimizing a linear function (straight line equation) subject to linear (straight line) constraints.

[23] George S. Yip, "Global Strategy in a World of Nations?," *Sloan Management review*, vol. 29 (Fall 1989), p. 33.

[24] The twelve components of this index are: institutions, infrastructure, macroeconomic stability, health and primary education, higher education and training, goods market efficiency, labor market efficiency, financial market sophistication, technological readiness, market size, business sophistication, and innovation. See World Economic Forum, *The Global Competitiveness Report 2007-2008*. Available at http://www.gcr.weforum.org/.

[25] The World Economic Forum defines competitiveness as ... the set of institutions, policies, and factors that determine the level of productivity of a country. The level of productivity, in turn, sets the sustainable level of prosperity that can be earned by an economy. In other words, more competitive economies tend to be able to produce higher levels of income for their citizens. The productivity level also determines the rates of return obtained by investments in an economy. Because the rates of return are the fundamental determinants of the growth rates of the economy, a more competitive economy is one that is likely to grow faster over the medium to long run. World Economic Forum, *Global Competitiveness Report*, chapter 1.1.

[26] International Management Development. World Competitiveness Yearbook, 2008. Scorecard available at http://www.imd.ch/research/publications/wcy/upload

[27] For details, see CRS Report RL34115, *Reform of U.S. International Taxation: Alternatives*, by Jane G. Gravelle. CRS Report RL31444, *Firms That Incorporate Abroad for Tax Purposes: Corporate "Inversions" and "Expatriation"*, by Donald J. Marples. U.S. Government Accountability Office, *International Taxation, Large U.S. Corporations and Federal Contractors with Subsidiaries in Jurisdictions Listed as Tax Havens or Financial Privacy Jurisdictions*, GAO- 09-157, December 18, 2008.

[28] Ng, Francis K. T., "Trends in average applied tariff rates in developing and industrial countries, 1981-2007," World Bank spreadsheet at *http://econ.world* bank.org/

WBSITE/EXTERNAL/EXTDEC/EXTRESEARCH/0,,contentMDK:21051044~pagePK:64214825~piPK:64214943~theSitePK:469382,00.html.

[29] See CRS Report RL32060, *World Trade Organization Negotiations: The Doha Development Agenda*, by Ian F. Fergusson.

[30] For a discussion of the effects of free-trade agreements, see CRS Report RL3 1356, *Free Trade Agreements: Impact on U.S. Trade and Implications for U.S. Trade Policy*, by William H. Cooper.

[31] See CRS Report RL33944, *Trade Primer: Qs and As on Trade Concepts, Performance, and Policy*, by Raymond J. Ahearn et al.

[32] CRS Report RL34330, *The Proposed U.S.-South Korea Free Trade Agreement (KORUS FTA): Provisions and Implications*, by William H. Cooper et al.

[33] Troy Stangarone, *Moving the KORUS FTA Forward in a Time of Economic Uncertainty* , Pacific Forum CSIS, PacNet No. 66, Honolulu, HI, December 11, 2008.

[34] Note that this analysis does not take into account possible offsetting effects to a change in trade flows induced by a tariff change. For example, increased exports could lead to a stronger dollar which then reduces U.S. exports.

[35] Numerous interviews by the author with businesses involved in global markets.

[36] Interviews by the author in 2006 and 2008 in Shanghai, China; Taipei, Taiwan; and Tokyo, Japan.

[37] CRS Report RL34561, *Foreign Investment and National Security: Economic Considerations*, by James K. Jackson. CRS Report RL33 103, *Foreign Investment in the United States: Major Federal Statutory Restrictions*, by Michael V. Seitzinger

[38] U.S. Bureau of Economic Analysis, *Foreign direct Investment in the U.S.: Country and Industry Detail for Capital Inflows, 2007*, accessed January 27, 2009.

[39] U.S. Bureau of Economic Analysis, *U.S. Direct Investment Abroad: Country and Industry Detail for Capital*, accessed January 27, 2009.

[40] See CRS Report RL34091, *Globalization, Worker Insecurity, and Policy Approaches*, by Raymond J. Ahearn.

[41] CRS Report RS21883, *Outsourcing and Insourcing Jobs in the U.S. Economy: An Overview of Evidence Based on Foreign Investment Data*, by James K. Jackson; CRS Report RL32292, *Offshoring (a.k.a. Offshore Outsourcing) and Job Insecurity Among U.S. Workers*, by Linda Levine.

[42] U.S. Bureau of Labor Statistics, "International Comparisons of Hourly Compensation Costs in Manufacturing, 2006," Economic News Release USDL: 08-0093, January 25, 2008.

[43] Michael E. Porter, "Clusters of Innovation, Regional Foundations of U.S. Competitiveness," Council on Competitiveness and the Monitor Group, October 2001, pp. 5-7.

[44] Booz Allen Hamilton, *China Manufacturing Competitiveness, 2007-2008* (Shanghai: American Chamber of Commerce in Shanghai, 2008), pp. 4, 13.

[45] The AFL-CIO, for example advocates the reform of trade rules to hold companies accountable for respecting workers' rights no matter where they produce and calls for the international community to recognize strong workers' rights and to incorporate obligations to uphold these fundamental rights in international rules and institutions. See AFL- CIO, "Policy Solutions to Shipping Jobs Overseas," accessed via Internet on September 15, 2008.

[46] See archived CRS Report RL31862, *Workplace Codes of Conduct in China and Related Labor Conditions*, by Thomas Lum.

[47] See U.S. Trade Representative, "Trade Facts, Bipartisan Agreement on Trade Policy," May 2007.

[48] See CRS Report RL34108, *U.S.-Peru Economic Relations and the U.S.-Peru Trade Promotion Agreement*, by M. Angeles Villarreal. For information on the International Labor Organization, see http://www.ilo.org/global/lang-en/ index.htm.

[49] See CRS Report RL34470, *A U.S.-Colombia Free Trade Agreement: Economic and Political Implications*, by M. Angeles Villarreal; CRS Report RL32540, *The Proposed U.S.-Panama Free Trade Agreement*, by J. F. Hornbeck; CRS Report RL34330, *The Proposed U.S.-South*

Korea Free Trade Agreement (KORUS FTA): Provisions and Implications, by William H. Cooper et al.; and CRS Report RL33743, *Trade Promotion Authority (TPA): Issues, Options, and Prospects for Renewal*, by J. F. Hornbeck and William H. Cooper.

50 U.S. Bureau of Labor Statistics.

51 Congressional Budget Office, *Factors Underlying the Decline in Manufacturing*, December 23, 2008, p. 6.

52 U.S. Department of Labor, Employment and Training Administration, *Trade Adjustment Assistance*, Fact Sheet, c.2008.

53 Congressional Budget Office, *Key Issues in Analyzing Major Health Insurance Proposals*, A CBO Study, Washington, DC, December 2008, p. 13.

54 Lee Hudson Teslik and Toni Johnson, *Healthcare Costs and U.S. Competitiveness*, Council on Foreign Relations, Backgrounder, Publication 13325, December 30, 2008.

55 General Motors. "About Us, Competitive Challenges, Health Care," GM 2006 Corporate Responsibility Report, 2006.

56 For further information, see, for example: CRS Report RL34389, *Health Insurance Reform and the 110th Congress*, by Jean Hearne. National Association of Manufacturers, *The NAM's Health Care Agenda*, Policy Issue Information/Human Resources Policy/ Health Care, accessed through Internet on January 2009.

57 For a European analysis of this issue, see EurActiv.com PLC. Fifth Report of the High Level Group on Competitiveness, Energy and The Environment, Contributing to an Integrated Approach to Competitiveness, Energy and Environment Policies, November 8, 2007. Available at http://ec.europa.eu/enterprise/. For a review of pertinent U.S. environmental law, see CRS Report RL30798, Environmental Laws: Summaries of Major Statutes Administered by the Environmental Protection Agency (EPA), by Susan R. Fletcher et al.

58 See, for example, CRS Report 98-738, *Global Climate Change: Three Policy Perspectives*, by Larry Parker and John Blodgett.

59 CRS Report R40100, *"Carbon Leakage" and Trade: Issues and Approaches*, by Larry Parker and John Blodgett.

60 For further information, see CRS Report RL30024, *U.S. Global Climate Change Policy: Evolving Views on Cost, Competitiveness, and Comprehensiveness*, by Larry Parker and John Blodgett; CRS Report RL30853, *Clean Air Act: A Summary of the Act and Its Major Requirements*, by James E. McCarthy et al.; CRS Report RL34762, *The National Ambient Air Quality Standard for Particulate Matter (PM): EPA's 2006 Revisions and Associated Issues*, by Robert Esworthy and James E. McCarthy; CRS Report RL34513, *Climate Change: Current Issues and Policy Tools*, by Jane A. Leggett; or CRS Report RL34659, *China's Greenhouse Gas Emissions and Mitigation Policies*, by Jane A. Leggett, Jeffrey Logan, and Anna Mackey.

61 CRS Report RS2 1625, *China's Currency: A Summary of the Economic Issues*, by Wayne M. Morrison and Marc Labonte.

62 For policy discussion, see CRS Report RL33206, *Vulnerability of Concentrated Critical Infrastructure: Background and Policy Options*, by Paul W. Parfomak; CRS Report RL31116, *Water Infrastructure Needs and Investment: Review and Analysis of Key Issues*, by Claudia Copeland and Mary Tiemann; CRS Report RL30153, *Critical Infrastructures: Background, Policy, and Implementation*, by John D. Moteff; CRS Report RL34567, *Public-Private Partnerships in Highway and Transit Infrastructure Provision*, by William J. Mallett; CRS Report RL34127, *Highway Bridges: Conditions and the Federal/State Role*, by Robert S. Kirk and William J. Mallett; and CRS Report RL33875, *Electric Transmission: Approaches for Energizing a Sagging Industry*, by Amy Abel.

63 Larry Rohter, "Shipping costs start to crimp globalization," *International Herald Tribune*. August 2, 2008.

64 David Blanchard, "The Latest Global Hotspot: The USA," *Industry Week*, October 2008, pp. 54-56.

65 Jonathan Katz, "Welcome Back U.S. Manufacturing," *Industry Week*, August 2008, pp. 34-37.

[66] U.S. Department of Transportation. MARAD. *Maritime Commerce Security Plan for the National Strategy for Maritime Security*, October 2005.

[67] See CRS Report RL33512, *Transportation Security: Issues for the 110th Congress*, by David Randall Peterman, Bart Elias, and John Frittelli. Also, see Department of Homeland Security, "DHS and DOE Launch Secure Freight Initiative," Press Release, December 7, 2006.

[68] Caldwell, Stephen L., "Supply Chain Security, Challenges to Scanning 100 Percent of U.S.-Bound Cargo Containers." Testimony Before the Subcommittee on Surface Transportation and Merchant Marine Infrastructure, Safety, and Security, Committee on Commerce, Science, and Transportation, U.S. Senate, GAO Report GAO-08-533T, June 12, 2008.

[69] Miller, John W.. "New Shipping Law Makes Big Waves In Foreign Ports," *Wall Street Journal*, October 25, 2007. pg. B.1.

[70] "Shanghai Port Grows as Trade Shrinks," *CargoNews Asia*, January 9, 2009.

[71] Interviews by the author with U.S. Consulate officials and business executives in Shanghai, China, February 2008.

[72] The American chamber of Commerce, People's Republic of China, *2008 White Paper, American Business in China*, 2008, pp. 105-106.

[73] Briefing of author in Singapore by the Ports Authority, August 2007.

[74] Zentralverband der Deutschen Seehafenbetriebe (German Seaport Operators), "Position Paper on House Resolution No. 1 (H.R. 1): Implementing Recommendations of the 9/11 Commission Act of 2007 – 100% Container Scanning. April 6, 2008.

[75] "US, EU reach cargo-screening agreement," *The Journal of Commerce Online*, October 31, 2008.

[76] For information on food safety, see CRS Report RL34198, *U.S. Food and Agricultural Imports: Safeguards and Selected Issues*, by Geoffrey S. Becker; CRS Report RL33472, *Sanitary and Phytosanitary (SPS) Concerns in Agricultural Trade*, by Geoffrey S. Becker.

[77] CRS Report RS21709, *Mad Cow Disease and U.S. Beef Trade*, by Charles E. Hanrahan and Geoffrey S. Becker.

[78] CRS Report RS22713, *Health and Safety Concerns Over U.S. Imports of Chinese Products: An Overview*, by Wayne M. Morrison.

[79] See http://www.fsis.usda.gov/About_FSIS/index.asp.

[80] See http://www.ncfpd.umn.edu/index.cfm.

[81] See CRS Report RL34539, *The U.S. Science and Technology Workforce*, by Deborah D. Stine and Christine M. Matthews.

[82] H.R. 2272 (1 10th Congress), America Competes Act (P.L. 110-69).

[83] For details, see CRS Report RL34292, *Intellectual Property Rights and International Trade*, by Shayerah Ilias and Ian F. Fergusson. CRS Report RL34593, *Infringement of Intellectual Property Rights and State Sovereign Immunity*, by Todd Garvey and Brian T. Yeh.

[84] CRS Report RS22880, *Intellectual Property Rights Protection and Enforcement: Section 337 of the Tariff Act of 1930*, by Shayerah Ilias.

[85] See CRS Report RL31832, *The Export Administration Act: Evolution, Provisions, and Debate*, by Ian F. Fergusson.

[86] U.S. Trade Representative, *2008 Special 301 Report*, Washington, DC, 2008, pp. 19-22. CRS Report RL33536, *China-U.S. Trade Issues*, by Wayne M. Morrison

[87] U.S. Trade Representative, 2008 Special 301 Report.

[88] John T. Mentzer, Matthew B. Myers, and Theodore P. Stank, *Handbook of Global Supply Chain Management* (Thousand Oaks, CA: Sage Publications, 2007), p. 23.

[89] CRS Report RL34683, *Taiwan-U.S. Relations: Recent Developments and Their Policy Implications*, by Kerry Dumbaugh.

[90] CRS Report 98-567, *The Overseas Private Investment Corporation: Background and Legislative Issues*, by Danielle Langton.

[91] Robert O'Harrow, Jr. and Brady Dennis , "The Beautiful Machine; Greed on Wall Street and blindness in Washington certainly helped cause the financial system's crash. But a deeper

explanation begins 20 years ago with a bold experiment to master the variable that has defeated so many visionaries: Risk. explanation begins 20 years ago with a bold experiment to master the variable that has defeated so many visionaries: Risk.," *Washington Post*, December 29, 2008; Brady Dennis and Robert O'Harrow, Jr. ,"A Crack in The System; 1998, AIG Financial Products had made hundreds of millions of dollars and had captured Wall Street's attention with its precise, finely balanced system for managing risk. Then it subtly turned in a dangerous direction ," *The Washington Post* , December 30, 2008.

[92] CRS Report 97-765, *The Buy American Act: Requiring Government Procurements to Come from Domestic Sources*, by John R. Luckey.

[93] World Trade Organization, *The Plurilateral Agreement on Government Procurement (GPA)*, Trade Topics, accessed January 15, 2009 [*http://www.wto.org/ english/ tratop_e/ gproc_e/gp_gpa_e.htm]*.

[94] U.S. Bureau of Economic Analysis, *U.S. Direct Investment Abroad* , *U.S. Parent Companies* , accessed December 30, 2008.

[95] Robert W. Hahn and Robert E. Litan, "Counting regulatory benefits and costs: lessons for the US and Europe," *Journal of International Economic Law 473–508*, vol. 8, no. 2 (June 2005), p. 473–508.

[96] See Office of Competition and Economic Analysis website at [http://www. ita. doc. gov/td/industry

[97] See USITC website at [http://www.usitc.gov/ind_econ_ana/index.htm].

[98] For information on the Congressional Budget Office, see [http://www.cbo.gov/aboutcbo/]/

[99] For information on the Council on Competitiveness, see [http://www.compete.org/].

[100] Elsie Echeverri-Carroll and Sofia G. Ayala, "Regulation and Competitiveness of U.S. Businesses: Is it time for a Competitiveness Impact Statement?," The University Of Texas At Austin, 2008.

[101] Ibid.

In: U.S. Trade, Protectionism and the Global... ISBN: 978-1-60876-966-7
Editors: Andrew J. Caldwell

Chapter 2

THE GLOBAL ECONOMIC DOWNTURN AND PROTECTIONISM

Raymond J. Ahearn

SUMMARY

In today's severe global economic downturn, concerns are being raised that countries may try to improve their own trade positions in order to help domestic industries at the expense of others by imposing measures that artificially increase their exports or restrict imports. Such efforts are considered by some to be a form of "protectionism" and are often referred to as beggar-thyneighbor policies.

This report develops three scenarios to approximate different dimensions of the relationship between the global economic downturn and protectionism. The scenarios are not predictions, but descriptions of how and why pressures for protection could be manifested and transmitted under different circumstances and assumptions.

Under a **low impact scenario,** existing World Trade Organization (WTO) rules and obligations, bolstered by a high level of global interdependence, discourage trade restrictions and trade diverting measures from being proposed. If implemented, the measures conform to WTO rules and/or have a limited impact on trade flows. Recent reports issued by the WTO and World Bank provide preliminary support for this scenario.

Under a **medium impact scenario,** WTO rules are violated or are disregarded due to the exigencies of the economic crisis and demands to provide financial rescue plans for the banking and auto sectors. As a result, trade and investment flows over time could be diverted or fall outside WTO surveillance, thereby weakening the global trading system.

Under a **high impact scenario,** WTO rules are violated, major trade conflict occurs, and the world trading system is undermined. This threat arises from the longstanding presence of large trade imbalances driven by distorted global consumption and savings patterns—patterns that were an underlying cause of the global economic downturn. Given the prominent role that China and the United States play in the global imbalances, two flashpoints for any outbreak of protectionism can be identified. The first could stem from U.S. public concerns that other countries are gaining a "free ride" in terms of international efforts to increase aggregate spending and get the world economy growing again. The second could arise if China and other surplus countries try to avoid massive factory closings and layoffs by exporting their overcapacity to the United States and Europe with trade policy measures such as export subsidies and currency depreciation.

Three broad policy challenges for Congress are derived from the analysis. The first deals with international surveillance of fiscal stimulus programs. The second relates to multilateral surveillance of trade pressures and barriers proposed and adopted during the economic crisis. The third pertains to the joint management of U.S. trade relations by Congress and the administration, particularly as it bears on responding to constituent requests for protection, facilitating the adjustment of current account surplus countries, and formulating trade liberalization priorities.

INTRODUCTION

The world economy may now be undergoing its most severe crisis since the Great Depression. The economies of the United States, Japan, and Europe are in recession and the emerging economies in Asia and Latin America are experiencing slower, if not negative, growth as well. According to the International Monetary Fund (IMF), world economic activity is projected to contract by 1/2 to 1 percent in 2009, the first such fall in 60 years.[1]

As economic activity has slowed around the globe and trade finance has become harder to obtain, world trade flows have also declined. The decline, which began in the summer of 2008, has affected all the major trading countries. Overall, the World Bank is predicting that world trade flows will decline by 2 percent in real terms in 2009 after growing by 4 percent in 2008. This may prove to be optimistic; early 2009 data show signs of sharper declines in export volumes, particularly among the open Asian export economies such as Singapore, Taiwan, and China.[2]

Emblematic of these concerns, the leaders of the most-developed G-20 countries proposed at a November 2008 meeting "to refrain from raising new barriers on trade in goods and services" for at least 12 months. Underlying this declaration was a view that government efforts to shield local companies from the global economic downturn through the imposition of trade barriers would only curb economic growth and prolong the global downturn. More starkly, there was an additional concern that a rise in trade barriers could turn the global downturn into a global depression. In the view of some analysts, this is what happened in the 1930s as a result of the passage of the U.S. Smoot-Hawley Tariff Act of 1930, an event which triggered a cycle of retaliation and counter-retaliation.

SMOOT-HAWLEY TARIFF ACT

The Smoot-Hawley Tariff Act of 1930 raised U.S. tariffs on over 20,000 products to an average level of 60 percent. After the U.S. passed the bill, other countries retaliated by raising their barriers to U.S. exports. World trade flows incurred a severe 66 percent drop between 1929 and 1934. Some economists argue that this huge drop in trade was what made the Depression great, by prolonging and deepening what had been a global recession. Other economists argue that U.S. tariffs were already quite high and that other factors such as misplaced faith in reliance on the gold standard and balanced budgets were bigger causes of the Great Depression. Greater consensus appears to exist on the notion that it is far better to keep markets open and increase world demand than to divert demand in national markets to domestic producers by raising trade barriers during a global recession.

The specter of widespread protectionism or trade wars currently is the subject of numerous newspaper and press articles.[3] Until recently it was possible to dismiss many mass media alarms on the grounds that today's global economy has numerous firewalls against protectionism that did not exist in the 1930s. But the accelerating global economic decline has increased pressures on policymakers to adopt a number of measures to assist distressed industries that are considered by some observers to be "protectionist."

Protectionism is a very elastic concept with multiple meanings. For many economists, no form of protection is legitimate because such interventions distort prices and misallocate resources over time. For some trade lawyers, only measures that are not consistent with WTO rules and obligations are protectionist and considered unacceptable. For many political realists and policymakers, protective measures that provide help to constituents in times of economic distress are a political responsibility and necessity, not protectionism. For some historians, efforts by countries to improve their own trade position and help domestic industries at the expense of others by imposing measures that artificially increase exports or limit imports describe protectionism. Still other historians define protectionism as a return to the policies of the 193 0s, which are characterized by substantial across the board increases in trade barriers often directed at particular countries and cycles of retaliation and counter-retaliation.

To analyze the relationship between the economic downturn and protectionism, this report constructs three scenarios. Each scenario reflects a different dimension of the relationship between the economic downturn and protectionism. The scenarios are a continuum based on an analysis of the situation today to the direction that trade protectionism could take under different assumptions and circumstances. The scenarios are not predictions, but descriptions of how and why protectionist pressures could be manifested and transmitted under very different situations and policy responses.

Under **a low impact scenario** existing WTO rules and obligations, bolstered by a high level of global interdependence, keep pressures for protection under control. Proposals for protection, if implemented, have a modest impact on global trade flows.

Under a **medium impact scenario** WTO rules prove inadequate or are disregarded due to the exigencies of the economic crisis. As a result, trade and investment flows over time could be diverted or fall outside WTO surveillance, thereby weakening the world trading system.

Under a **high impact scenario** WTO rules are violated or ignored, major trade conflicts occur, and the world trading system is damaged. This threat arises from longstanding trade imbalances driven by distorted global savings and consumption patterns.

The depth and duration of the economic downturn likely will be a major determinant of which scenario or scenarios prevail. At the same time, the degree to which protectionist measures are adopted could affect the course of the economic downturn as well.

A concluding section discusses several policy challenges that rising pressures for trade protection may pose for policymakers and the 111th Congress. This issue is also bound to be on the agenda of the G-20 countries when the leaders meet in London on April 2, 2009 to coordinate responses to the global economic crisis.

LOW IMPACT SCENARIO: FIREWALLS HOLD AS WTO RULES AND OBLIGATIONS CONSTRAIN PROTECTIONIST MEASURES

There are a number of reasons why the threat of a return to protectionist, beggar-thy-neighbor policies could be vastly overstated. Unlike the 1930s, today's global economy has several strong firewalls to prevent governments from raising trade barriers that result in a cycle of retaliation and counter-retaliation. These firewalls include more institutionalized obstacles to protectionism built into the WTO system, more policy instruments to address the economic slowdown, and a more interdependent and open world economy than existed in the 1930s.

In addition, some in today's media may tend to overstate the threat of protectionism by not always distinguishing between protectionist actions and protectionist pressures and/or by equating legitimate forms of protection with protectionism. The fact that there is ample room for increases in trade measures and barriers that are consistent with the rules and obligations of the WTO often may go unappreciated in some press coverage. These trade measures and barriers include increases in applied tariffs to bound rates, and imposition of countervailing and antidumping duties, so-called 'defensive' trade measures.[4] Protection for limited periods of time and under prescribed conditions is built into the rules of the WTO as a political safety valve and as a recognition of the human and social costs that are associated with the often wrenching adjustments that accompany increased trade competition.

Firewalls against Protectionism

WTO rules today serve to keep a lid on trade barriers of its 153 members through an elaborate set of mutual obligations and dispute settlement procedures. Unlike the 1930s when countries could impose higher trade barriers unilaterally without violating any international agreements or anticipating a foreign reaction, under today's rules members can take their disputes to the WTO for settlement rather than engaging in reciprocal retaliatory actions. The fact that countries violating WTO obligations can face WTO-sanctioned retaliation helps constrain outbreaks of unilateral actions that could be mutually harmful.[5]

Pressures for protection are also dampened by a world economy that is much more interdependent and integrated than in the 1930s.[6] Leading producers have become so international in their production operations and supply chains that they have developed a vested interest in resisting protectionism.[7] Many industries that have faced import competition in the past – such as televisions and semiconductors—have found that international diversification or joint ventures with foreign partners are a more profitable way of coping with global competition than blocking goods at the border. In addition, many domestic industries have less incentive to ask for import restrictions because foreign rivals now produce in the domestic market, eliminating the benefits of trade barriers for domestic firms.[8]

Unlike the early 1930s, when governments took little responsibility for propping up financial institutions and were unable to pursue expansionary monetary policies due to fixed exchange rates under the gold standard, policymakers around the world today are adopting expansionary fiscal and monetary policies. These expansionary policies, in turn, have the capability of dampening protectionist pressures and demands that stem from job losses and related economic hardship with lower interest rates and increased expenditures on unemployment benefits and health care benefits.[9]

A related consideration is that today's world economy is much more open than the world economy of the 193 0s. Average tariffs on world trade have come down from the 50% range in the 1930s, to the 25% range in the 1980s, and to less than 10% today.[10] Under these circumstances, it would require tremendous increases in protection to get the world back to anywhere near the conditions of the 1930s, although a major increase in tariffs (e.g. a doubling) would be disruptive even if it left tariffs well below the 1930s levels.

Scorecard of Protective Measures to Date

Empirical support exists for the view that existing legal, economic, and political firewalls are restraining today's protectionist pressures. Most importantly, Pascal Lamy, the WTO's Director General, reported in January 2009 that most WTO members have successfully kept domestic protectionist pressures under control "with only limited evidence of increases in trade restricting or trade distorting measures" taken during the last six months of 2008. This assessment was based on the first report of the WTO secretariat on the trade effects of the global economic crisis. The report found only "limited evidence" of an increase in tariffs, non-tariff barriers or trade-remedy actions by member countries, but noted that the most significant actions taken in response to the global crisis have involved "financial support of one kind or another to banks and other financial institutions and to certain industries, notably the automobile industry."[11]

The WTO report notes tariff increases on selected products being implemented by India, Russia, Ecuador, and Ukraine. Countries adopting non-tariff measures include Indonesia (port of entry barriers) and Argentina (import licensing requirements). Argentina was cited for measures that attempt to boost exports of selected products. But the report indicates that there has been "no dramatic increase" in antidumping investigations in the second half of 2008 compared to first half of 2008, but raised the possibility of increased trade remedy actions in 2009.[12]

The World Bank, which has also been monitoring trade restrictions proposed and adopted since the beginning of the financial crisis, reached a conclusion similar to that of the WTO. Its initial report determined that there have been 47 trade restrictive measures imposed since the financial crisis began last summer, including 17 from G-20 countries, but that "these measures have probably had only marginal effects on trade flows to date." In addition to the measures cited by the WTO, the World Bank report cited China's import ban on various food products from the EU, and export subsidies provided by the EU, China, and India. Contrary to the WTO report, the World Bank report determined that "the number of antidumping cases (both investigations initiated and imposition of duties) surged in 2008."[13]

Proposals Modified

Further support for the "firewalls are holding" perspective can also be found in the evolution of proposals for protection that have been either modified or withdrawn. The two most prominent cases that fit this description are a Buy American provision contained in the U.S. stimulus legislation (P.L. 111-5, Sec. 1 605),[14] and a French proposal to require its carmakers to produce and source locally.

As originally passed by the House on January 28, 2009, the stimulus bill contained a provision that would have required the use of U.S. iron and steel for infrastructure projects funded by the bill. The Senate's amended version of the provision, which prevailed in conference, went further in requiring the use of U.S. manufactured goods (in addition to iron and steel) in specified projects, but also included language requiring that the provision had to be implemented in a manner consistent with U.S. international trade obligations. This language was vigorously supported by U.S. multinational companies and trading partners such as the European Union and Canada.

Some observers maintain that the Buy American provision agreed to in the stimulus bill may have only a very limited impact on international trade flows. This is because the law waives Buy American restrictions according to a number of broad public interest tests, including if "the relevant manufactured goods are not produced in the United States in sufficient and reasonably available quantities." With imported goods now comprising nearly 40% of all manufactured goods sold in the United States, imports in a large number of areas may not be constrained.[15]

Supporters also say the Buy American provision is the kind of measure that is often dubbed "protectionist" on questionable grounds. Up until 1979, when the Tokyo Round of trade negotiations reached agreement on a voluntary Agreement on Government Procurement (AGP), government procurement was entirely excluded from international trading system obligations. Today only 39 of 153 WTO members have joined the AGP, an agreement that opens up government procurement according to negotiated sectors, agencies, and thresholds. The limited nature of the AGP reflects, in part, the fact that government procurement decisions are still viewed largely as a means of achieving legitimate domestic policy goals, including increasing the probability that public spending will generate domestic jobs.[16]

Opponents dispute the claims that this provision may have a small impact on international trade and is not "protectionist." A key assertion is that many major U.S. trading partners that are not signatories to the AGP, such as Brazil,

China, and India, will face discrimination in bidding on the projects covered by the law. Facing such discrimination, these countries may decide to retaliate by pressuring their companies perhaps to buy from European producers instead of U.S. suppliers or by pursuing their own buy-national policies. For example, while China recently removed from one of its recent stimulus bills a provision instructing "governments of different levels to give priority to home-grown light-industry products," the mere public introduction of the clause reportedly has been enough to get provincial authorities to favor local over foreign suppliers in the procurement of a broad range of products.[17]

The French government's decision in February 2009 to provide $3.9 billion in preferential loans to Renault and Peugeot-Citroen was similarly controversial due to buy-local or buy-national concerns. As a condition for the loans, it was initially reported that the French government was requiring these two automakers to source from French suppliers and to close factories in other countries to ensure that car factories located in France keep operating. This apparent effort to prevent outsourcing of French car production provoked a strong reaction from the Czech Republic and Slovakia, countries where Peugeot-Citroen had factories. The Czech Republic immediately called for an emergency European summit to protest France's "protectionist plan" and the European Commission (EC) agreed to investigate what appeared to be a violation the EU's single market rules.[18] After weeks of discussion with the EC, French authorities pledged not to implement measures that would breach the principles of the single market by requiring manufacturing activities to be maintained in France.[19]

Medium Impact Scenario: WTO Rules Prove Inadequate, Particularly for Sector-Specific Assistance, and Trading System Is Weakened

Under this scenario, WTO rules and obligations are disregarded or prove ineffective and trade and capital flows are diverted or misallocated. As a result, the global trading system could be weakened over time.

This scenario involves sector specific financial assistance programs that governments around the world have developed in response to the economic crisis. To date these programs have been directed primarily to auto companies and banks. In the auto sector, almost every producing country—the United States, Canada, Sweden, Germany, France, Australia, Argentina, Brazil, South

Korea, and China – has launched programs to aid producers or stimulate car sales. One estimate totals these subsidies at $48 billion worldwide, including $17.4 billion thus far in the United States. In the financial services sector, the WTO reports that 58 different programs worth trillions of dollars have been announced by 26 countries in an effort to strengthen struggling institutions.[20]

These financial assistance programs have been devised and implemented in response to extraordinary conditions. In the financial sector, as some major banks and institutions have appeared on the edge of bankruptcy, government rescue packages and takeovers have increased in scope and magnitude in an effort to avoid contagion or systematic risk—not by a desire to save failing companies. The destruction of wealth in the financial sector has also hurt the real economy and key industrial sectors, with large firms facing bankruptcy and large cut-backs in their labor force.

While alleged subsidies contained in the rescue packages under some circumstances can improve national economic performance and resource allocation, they may also be a vehicle for a kind of murky protection and misallocation of resources. Whether any of the many different rescue packages discriminate against foreign firms may also become an important consideration in judging their impact on the trading system over time.[21]

Auto Sector Rescue Programs

Slumping sales and employment have led the major auto producing countries to adopt or consider a range of financial assistance programs. The measures vary in the degree to which they help companies directly through loans and guarantees or indirectly through tax incentives and credits for buying new cars. The programs also differ to the extent they try to insure that only domestic companies may benefit. Because many of these programs are still evolving or lack publicly- announced details, the trade consequences are mostly speculative.

Some experts have argued that these assistance programs could be challenged as violations of the subsidies rules under the WTO Agreement on Subsidies and Countervailing Measures (ASCM). Under Article 3 of the ASCM, subsidies that are contingent upon export performance or upon the use of domestic over imported goods are prohibited. Countries could also challenge another country's assistance programs on the grounds that loans were not provided on a commercial basis. However, such a challenge would also need to prove that trade injury occurred (either "serious prejudice" or a "threat of serious prejudice") to car producers of other WTO signatories. This could prove a difficult hurdle since several years of evidence are required to show that imports have been displaced or impeded, prices have been suppressed or undercut, and imports have lost market share.[22]

As a practical matter, many observers think that WTO cases are unlikely to be filed. This is because a country bringing the challenge could expect that its own auto industry assistance program could be similarly challenged. Considerable cross-ownership of companies complicates such filings as well. In addition, foreign carmakers operating in the United States, such as Toyota and Honda, may be unwilling to support any WTO complaint given that they have received tax- breaks or subsidies to build factories from U.S. state governments.[23]

Foreign auto-assistance measures such as loans or loan guarantees could also be challenged under each country's countervailing duty (CVD) laws.[24] If successful, countervailing duties could be imposed to offset any competitive advantages that an auto exporting company may have received from its government. Such cases must meet similar tests to a challenge under the ASCM, but it is the industry, rather than the government, that would bring a case. While it could be easier to obtain an affirmative finding in a countervailing duty case because national authorities, not WTO panels, make the injury determinations, these cases can take up to two to three years to resolve. Assuming a duty eventually was imposed on imported autos, a car company in the targeted country could file a similar case against the country that imposed the duty.[25] If the CVD cases proved successful, subsidies may stay in place and generate inefficient production over time, with world trade in autos becoming more fragmented and protected.[26]

Other concerns have been raised beyond trade diversion. One is that the various subsidy packages being implemented around the world may not only strain national budgets, but also result in a misallocation of resources. Firms that have access to the largest subsidies, under this perspective, will be able to ride out the global economic downturn longer, raising concern that access to state funds rather than commercial viability determines success.[27]

Another concern is that more industries will be encouraged to lobby for preferential financing, encouraging a subsidy race in other sectors. For example, auto parts manufacturers in some countries are now requesting assistance similar to what the automakers have received.

A final concern is that the auto industry could become isolated from WTO rules and disciplines, similar to the situation in the shipbuilding and steel industries. Under this perspective, if countries set up their own criteria for permissible subsidies with little regard for market conditions, the world trading system could be weakened.[28]

Financial Sector Rescue Programs

As the financial crisis has spread over the world, governments have launched extensive rescue programs for troubled banks and other institutions, along with other monetary and fiscal policy initiatives. For example, Iceland has nationalized all its major banks, and the United Kingdom has taken a 68% share of the Royal Bank of Scotland.[29] The United States has taken control over Fannie Mae and Freddie Mac and has extended billions of dollars to American International Group (AIG) and Citigroup.[30] In U.S. cases, the government has received interest or equity stakes in return for assistance with the subsidy element taking the form of more favorable terms and financing than the companies could receive on the open market.

From a trade perspective, a concern is that some governments, like Britain, are directing their banks with global operations to lend to domestic companies and citizens before providing loans to foreigners. While these actions may not violate any international legal obligations (WTO rules regulating assistance to financial institutions lag behind those regulating assistance to goods producers), this form of financial protectionism may undermine the spirit of globalization that supports an open world trading system.[31] At the same time, it can be noted that there has been substantial international cooperation in the financial sphere among the key central banks of the world to deal with the financial crisis.

High Impact Scenario: WTO Rules Are Violated, Major Trade Conflicts Occur, and Trading System Is Undermined

Under this scenario, WTO rules are violated or ignored and major trade conflicts occur. As a result, the functioning and legitimacy of the world trading system is undermined.

This threat arises from the longstanding presence of highly skewed trade balances driven by distorted global consumption and savings patterns—patterns that were an underlying cause of the global economic downturn. High savings countries such as China, Japan and Germany produced more than they consumed and had to rely on export-led growth to help keep their economies growing. In the process, these three countries, plus the oil-exporting countries, experienced large and growing current account surpluses.[32] In 2008, the current account surpluses were estimated to be around $2 trillion.[33] The United States, on the other hand, was a low savings country, consuming much and having to borrow from the rest of the world to finance its investment needs.

Re-balancing Trade Flows

Overall trade imbalances are caused by different international savings and investment levels. Much of the earnings of the current account surplus countries were recycled to U.S. capital markets in the form of purchases of U.S. securities, helping make capital abundant and cheap in the United States.[34] Cheap and abundant capital, in turn, facilitated rising levels of U.S. consumption and investment in housing.[35] When U.S. consumption began to contract due to the rapid decline in housing prices and the credit crisis, the pattern of global trade and financial flows was no longer tenable.[36]

Policies that correct the imbalances and provide for more balanced growth in the next decade are important both for a global economic recovery and an avoidance of an outbreak of trade conflict. For current account deficit countries like the United States, where domestic spending exceeds current production, spending must decline and savings rise. This can be achieved by a reduction of consumption or investment (or a combination of both).[37] This, of course, is happening quickly in the United States with rising unemployment and the credit crunch forcing drastic reductions in domestic spending, particularly investment spending.[38] The U.S. current account deficit has now begun to fall, from 6% of GDP in 2006 to 4.5% in 2008, and possibly to 3% or even 2% in 2009.[39]

For the current account surplus countries, the rapid U.S. adjustment means that they will have to sustain their growth more by stimulating domestic demand and less by net exports. For these countries, where domestic spending is less than current production, domestic spending will need to rise. This, in turn, can be accomplished by increases in consumption, investment, or government spending (or a combination of all three). While expansive government spending programs or higher domestic consumption generally are the preferred path for the demand increases to take place, sharp reductions in supply or production in current account surplus countries are also possible. For example, China, the largest current account surplus country, would have to be able to increase its consumption to an estimated 17% of GDP—a 40% expansion—to offset the expected decline in U.S. consumption of 5% of GDP. It has been argued that this would be a huge adjustment, and one that is perhaps beyond the ability of government spending programs alone to stimulate.[40] Given the prominent role that China and the United States play in the global imbalances, two flashpoints for any outbreak of protectionism can be identified. The first involves the possibility that some countries could be perceived as "free riders" in the international effort to increase global aggregate demand. The second relates to the daunting task many countries, particularly China, Japan and Germany, face in shifting their economies towards a greater reliance on domestic demand.

Dealing with Fiscal Stimulus "Free Riders"

This flashpoint stems from the need for an increase in global aggregate demand to rescue the world economy from a continuing downward slide. To offset retrenchments in private consumption, investment, and exports and to avoid the trade imbalances of the past, countries are being urged to adopt coordinated fiscal stimulus packages. But some concerns have emerged in the United States, which has adopted a $787 billion stimulus program, over the size and composition of the plans and commitments of other G-20 countries.[41] These concerns have been directed primarily towards China and some European countries.[42]

China, which adopted a $585 billion stimulus program in November 2008, has been urged to spend more given its huge holdings of foreign reserves, as well as to make its spending more transparent. For example, it is unclear how much of the spending from China's November stimulus will be new expenditures versus already announced plans. Plus it is unclear how much of the new spending will benefit industrial development and China's exporting industries versus consumers and domestic demand.[43]

France, the United Kingdom, and Germany are European countries that some observers believe could be doing more to support world demand. According to IMF staff estimates (**Table 1**), their stimulus packages as a percent of GDP tend to lag behind the U.S. and Chinese plans.

These European countries counter that the relative size of various stimulus packages need to account for spending on automatic stabilizers such as unemployment benefits, health care, and training. Given that European countries tend to have larger such expenditures, an IMF analysis taking these expenditures into account indicates much stronger contributions to global demand are being made by Germany, the United Kingdom and Italy and a much weaker contribution being made by China (see **Table 2**).

Table 1. Stimulus Packages in Large Countries (in percent of GDP)

	2008	2009	2010	Total
United States	1.1	2.0	1.8	4.8
China	0.4	2.0	2.0	4.4
Germany	0.0	1.5	2.0	3.4
Canada	0.0	1.5	1.3	2.7
Japan	0.4	1.4	0.4	2.2
United Kingdom	0.2	1.4	-0.1	1.5
France	0.0	0.7	0.7	1.3
India	0.0	0.5	....	0.5
Italy	0.0	0.2	0.1	0.3
Average	0.5	1.6	1.3	3.4

Source: International Monetary Fund, "The Size of the Fiscal Expansion: An Analysis for the Largest Countries," Fiscal Affairs Department, February 2009.

Notes: PPP GDP-weighted average.

Table 2. Change in Overall Fiscal Balance (in percent of GDP, relative to pre-crisis year 1/)

	2008	2009	2010	Average
United States	-3.5	-5.7	-6.1	-5.1
Germany	....	-3.2	-4.4	-3.8
United Kingdom	-1.5	-4.6	-5.4	-3.8
Japan	-1.3	-3.7	-3.7	-2.9
India	-2.6	-3.3	-2.2	-2.7
Canada	-0.9	-2.9	-3.2	-2.4
China	-1.1	-3.0	-3.0	-2.3
France	-0.6	-2.8	-3.6	-2.3
Italy	-1.1	-2.4	-2.8	-2.1

Source: International Monetary Fund, "The Size of the Fiscal Expansion: An Analysis for the Largest Countries."

Notes: Pre-crisis year is 2007, except for Germany (2008).

The IMF analysis also points out that due to already large public debt, some countries, like India, Italy, and Japan, have less "fiscal space" or leeway to undertake expansionary fiscal policies. In addition, some countries may be reluctant to undertake a fiscal expansion because the recession is not yet deep for them. And some developing countries may be unable to use fiscal stimulus because of fears that investors will lose confidence in their credit worthiness. Moreover, in every polity, including the United States, there are stakeholders opposed to the use of expansionary fiscal policy on the grounds that it either won't work or will pass on to future generations debt that current citizens should pay.

While the United States is the world's largest economy and perhaps the only one capable of increasing global demand quickly, it is no longer large enough to be the single locomotive of the world economy or the global consumer of last resort. Because stimulus in any country will boost demand for both domestically produced goods and imports, the United States needs help from the other trade surplus countries to spur its exports and economic growth at a time when its spending and consumption are being diffused to help countries like China that are the world's major producers. Absent such help, some observers say protectionist pressures could grow in the United States if the large U.S. stimulus increases U.S. indebtedness by far more than it increases demand for U.S. goods.[44] Stated differently, if the U.S. economy after a year or two has little to show for running expansionary policies and incurring increased public debt—for example, unemployment remains high, there is little or no economic recovery, and the increased public debt begins to weaken the value of the dollar[45]—the American public may ask why such a large share of U.S. stimulus spending is leaking abroad and generating jobs in countries that have not stimulated their own economies sufficiently to increase imports of U.S. products.[46]

The fiscal policies of the countries with large external surpluses, thus, are critical for the world economy to recover in a timely manner and, over time become more balanced in terms of spending patterns relative to production. In a deep recession, some analysts maintain that failure of the current account surplus countries to increase domestic demand in a substantial manner is a form of a beggar-thy-neighbor policy as they import demand from the rest of the world. According to this perspective, current account surplus countries are also exporting their unemployment to the rest of the world and "cannot be surprised if deficit countries even resort to protectionist measures."[47] Interestingly, the United States was the world's largest current account surplus country in the 1930s, and, thus, was essentially in China's position today.

UNITED STATES AND CURRENT ACCOUNT SURPLUSES IN THE 1930S

The trade and financial imbalances that were an underlying cause of today's global economic crisis were in some ways similar to the imbalances that characterized the world economy in the 1 920s and 1 930s. During this period, the United States was the largest current account surplus country, financing the deficits of countries in Europe with capital exports through bonds floated by foreign countries in New York. These capital exports allowed a number of European countries to continue to run large deficits, while the United States continued expanding its industrial capacity. The financial crisis of 1929-31 led to a collapse of the bond market, effectively cutting off funding for the current account deficit countries and their ability to buy U.S. goods. This drop in foreign demand, in turn, forced the United States to either increase domestic demand or cut back on domestic production. But instead of running an expansionary fiscal policy (increasing domestic demand), the United States cut back spending and then in 1930 enacted the Smoot-Hawley Tariff. The trade deficit nations retaliated, raised their own tariffs, and world trade collapsed. This forced most of the global adjustment (deep production cuts and high unemployment) on the United States and other current account surplus countries in Latin America. Deficit countries such as Germany, Italy, and Spain suffered much less. (Most economists think that the main reason the Depression was milder in some countries was due to the fact that they abandoned the gold standard more quickly than the United States, thereby giving them greater flexibility to run expansionary fiscal policies). One tentative implication is that if today's crisis were to lead to a trade war, all countries would be worse off, but surplus countries, especially China, would suffer the most. Source: Michael Pettis, "Asia Faces a Tough 2009 as Output Decreases," *Financial Times,* December 15, 2008, and Martin Wolf, "What Obama Should Tell the Leaders of the Group of 20," *Financial Times,* February 25, 2009.

Current Account Surplus Countries – Transitioning to Domestic- Led Growth

A second flashpoint relates to the task that many countries, particularly China, Japan, and Germany, face in shifting their economies towards greater reliance on domestic demand – that is producing more for themselves rather than exporting to the rest of the world. Stated differently, these countries need to reduce their heavy reliance on exports by reorienting their economies more towards domestic consumption and investment. But for a variety of cultural, political and economic reasons, the transition may be extremely difficult.

In the case of China, efforts to increase consumption and domestic demand will not be easy or quick. Chinese households, for example, have one of the highest savings rates in the world (up to 25%). Chinese families, especially those in rural areas, save at such high rates because they receive little government support with education costs, medical care, and retirement. The average hospital stay can cost the equivalent of two years wages for the average Chinese worker. In addition, some of the items Chinese people may want to consume are not necessarily the goods being produced for export. Some production, thus, may need to be re-engineered and some workers retrained and re-deployed because China's economy biases the economy towards exports rather than domestic consumption. Yet, requests from factory managers to make goods for the domestic market may take up to two years for all the necessary approvals to be made. Moreover, lending of the Chinese banking system continues to be biased towards boosting manufacturing and infrastructure projects, not consumer spending.[48]

Japan's longstanding export dependence has been fueled by a mind-set of export or perish. Based on a shortage of natural resources, most Japanese have adopted a mercantilist perspective tied to the notion that Japan's power is dependent upon exporting manufactured goods in exchange for raw materials and generating trade surpluses with the rest of the world. This mind-set has been bolstered by a banking system that places priority on allocating credit to big exporting companies.

Given that Japan's economy declined by 3% in the last quarter of 2008, there may be added urgency for the government to undertake additional spending programs. For such spending to generate increases in private demand, much of the new money would have to be channeled to education, housing, and improving Japan's health care infrastructure. Hundreds of thousands of small- and medium-sized businesses, which employ two-thirds of Japan's workforce, stand to benefit from a redirection of credit.[49] At the same time, Japan has had interest rates near zero for several years and still has been unable to stimulate domestic demand.

Germany's economy is heavily dependent on the world economy for its growth as well. It is the world's largest exporter of goods and 25% of its jobs are export dependent. Moreover, it has objected to implementing larger spending programs on historical and structural grounds. Savings were wiped out by policies that created hyperinflation in the 1920s and German economic policy, ever since the end of World War II, has emphasized stability over economic growth. Opposition to additional spending, thus, is rooted in both fears of its inflationary impact, plus concerns that additional debt could be a drag on growth in the future. Because the economic crisis to date has had few palpable effects on ordinary Germans (except for their automobile industry), efforts to induce already high saving Germans to spend any extra cash could prove difficult.[50]

Assuming the transition to domestic-led growth by China takes years to accomplish, a major concern is that the current account surplus countries could try to avoid massive factory closings by resorting to tariff and trade policies designed to export their overcapacity to the rest of the world. This concern was highlighted by one Chinese trade official who recently stated that "China will resort to tariff and trade policies to facilitate exports of labor-intensive and core technology- supported industries."[51]

Providing export subsidies, increasing import tariffs, and depreciating a currency were the tools most often utilized in the 193 0s to boost exports. As the history of this period demonstrated, countries cannot all export their way to growth unless they collectively act to boost imports. Without an import boost, trade tensions will likely escalate and possibly lead to serious trade conflicts.

POLICY CHALLENGES FOR CONGRESS

The global economic downturn is deep and broad. Job cuts and declining levels of economic activity are affecting countries around the globe. Even before the crisis hit, there had been an erosion of public support for trade and globalization in many countries, including the United States. As a result, increased pressures for protection should not be unexpected.

Policymakers and Members of Congress, thus, find themselves situated between a rock and a hard place. On the one hand, they are under increased pressure to respond to pleas from voters to take action that will alleviate immediate distress. On the other hand, they are cognizant of the need to keep markets open and trade and investment flowing. How to balance considerations of constituent requests for relief—national and political demands—with recognition of the growing imperatives of an integrated global economy—which requires international cooperation—is an overarching dilemma.

In this context, three broad policy challenges can be derived from the analysis presented in this report. The first deals with international coordination and surveillance of fiscal stimulus programs. The second relates to multilateral surveillance of trade pressures and barriers adopted during this crisis. The third pertains to the management of U.S. trade relations, particularly as it relates to trade with China and other current account surplus countries.

Coordination and Surveillance of Stimulus Programs

Most economists maintain that governments need to place high priority on bolstering aggregate demand in an effort to arrest deteriorating economic conditions around the world. Expansionary economic policies, via tax cuts, increased public spending, and budget deficits, are one way to get national and global economic activity moving again. In addition to its beneficial impact on bolstering global demand and addressing the recession, such policies can also be channeled to alleviating some of the losses (jobs and health care benefits) workers are experiencing from the economic downturn—losses that often intensify protectionist pressures.

Expansionary policies, including monetary policies, are not universally supported. Some critics worry about consequences of larger public debt. Many European governments maintain that financial regulatory reforms are a more important priority.[52] Other critics believe that it is more efficient to allow markets to adjust without government interference. And still others maintain that expansionary policies are unlikely to prove sufficient in achieving long-term rebalancing of domestic demand.

The current account surplus countries generally are in the best position to run expansionary fiscal policies.[53] Such policies are also necessary if current account deficit countries, which are trying to save more than before, are able to improve their net export position, a development critical for economic recovery. Moreover, the United States, the world's largest deficit country, will be hard pressed to employ expansionary economic policies for many years without adverse consequences for the value of the dollar and its overall debt position. In the absence of help from these countries, political frustration in the United States could grow if it is perceived that other countries are shirking their global economic responsibilities.

Under these circumstances, it could prove helpful if policymakers and Members of Congress had available an objective analysis of the extent to which all major countries are pursuing expansionary policies, given their differential circumstances. Such public information could be used in discussions with their counterparts (in all major countries) to do their "fair" share in keeping the world economy moving forward and as a way to hold everyone to account. The analysis could include targets for demand growth and monetary policy, perhaps differentiated by individual country circumstances. U.S. Treasury Secretary Tim Geithner has called for each G20 country to set a spending target equaling 2 percent of aggregate GDP for 2009 and 2010, and for the IMF to monitor progress towards that goal.[54] Some economists are calling for a more ambitious 3 percent spending target given the deterioration in the outlook for world economic growth.[55]

The IMF's Fiscal Affairs Department has produced an analysis that addresses this objective in part. Whether such an analysis or macroeconomic scorecard could benefit from a formal mandate from the leadership of the IMF or the G-20 countries is something that could be considered.[56]

Multilateral Surveillance of Trade Barriers

The WTO Secretariat has begun tracking trade and trade-related measures taken in the context of the current economic crisis. These efforts are designed to bolster policymakers' resolve to reject calls for protection by making the measures transparent and public. The idea is that by raising public awareness of what barriers are being imposed, countries may realize that they are not acting alone and that their restrictive measures could be emulated quickly by their trading partners.[57]

An initial concern about the WTO effort is that the data have been drawn primarily from secondary sources such as press reports. Member governments currently are obliged to notify the WTO about changes in applied tariffs and subsidies only on an annual basis. For the tracking system to become more useful and relevant, there may be a need for greater involvement of member governments in providing information on new measures adopted. Along with this information, the member country could be asked to provide some justification for taking the action, along with a promise to remove the new protection within a certain period of time.

It also has been suggested that an inventory of new protective measures, many of which are likely to be WTO-consistent or legal, could also prove useful once the global recession ends. Much of the damage from the higher tariffs of the 193 0s was that they remained in place for decades. Thus, devising a plan to remove the barriers induced during the economic crisis arguably could also be contemplated.[58]

Management of U.S. Trade Relations

The global economic downturn creates numerous challenges for Congress and the President in managing U.S. trade relations. Based on a longstanding division of responsibilities -- Congress's constitutional responsibility to "regulate foreign commerce" and presidential responsibility to negotiate with foreign countries—the legislative and executive branches of government are challenged to consult and cooperative closely. This is true on a range of issues, including constituent requests for protection, facilitating the adjustment of current account surplus countries, and formulating trade liberalization priorities.

Responding to requests for protection

As constituent requests for protection are likely to increase as the recession persists, Congress is faced with balancing the political imperative of being responsive to constituent needs against U.S. international obligations under the WTO. On the one hand, current WTO and other international trade obligations do grant member countries some leeway to raise tariffs, protect domestic producers for limited periods of time, and provide domestic preferences or financial assistance to specific sectors under certain circumstances. Such protection provides a political safety valve for absorbing the political pressures associated with efforts of companies and workers to adjust to increased competition. On the other, protection that falls outside existing international trade obligations has less legitimacy. Under these circumstances, the policy challenge is not necessarily protection versus no protection, but under what circumstances might protection be appropriate and for how long. As the history of U.S. trade policy suggests, providing no protection when it may be warranted can often backfire, generating support for greater and perhaps excessive protection at a later date.[59]

Dealing with current account surplus countries

How best to facilitate a more rapid adjustment of current account surplus countries is a second large challenge for Congress and the Executive Branch. Legislative initiatives threatening trade sanctions, for example, are likely to hurt both sides if imposed, but they could also provide the President with useful leverage in pressing counterparts in Europe and Asia to do more in terms of boosting aggregate demand.

In an ideal world, international cooperation and institutions are a better way to encourage the current account surplus countries to undertake necessary structural changes and to head off protectionist actions. As part of any agreement, a realistic amount of time may be required for these countries to make the necessary adjustments. In return for open markets in the deficit countries while these changes are being made, the surplus countries could agree not to employ predatory trade policies.[60]

Problems and possible conflict likely will occur, however, if it becomes clear that current account surplus countries are trying to export their overcapacity and unemployment to the United States by manipulating their exchange rate, subsidizing exports, or blocking imports.[61] Challenging these practices through the available international channels may be less politically contentious and more effective than unilateral actions, but such challenges can often take years to be resolved. In the meantime, trade can take on a zero sum game appearance as the choice between preserving jobs at home or abroad becomes more stark.

Considering the role of trade liberalization

A third challenge for the Congress and Administration involves weighing the role that trade liberalizing agreements can play during the current recession. On the one hand, in a time of great economic uncertainty and retrenchment, many stakeholders may prefer to preserve benefits (subsidies or tariffs) that they already have. This is because trade liberalization rests on a willingness to swap current benefits derived by protection or subsidies in return for future benefits offered by promises of greater access to foreign markets that are growing. On the other hand, trade liberalization, by cutting protection, may provide an effective economic stimulus and, in the process, appear more attractive. As the economic downturn has placed added demands on the use of public funds to stimulate economic activity, conducting negotiations that free up public funds through the reduction of subsidies may become more appealing.

One key practical question is whether the global economic downturn could cast the long-stalled Doha Round of multilateral negotiations in a new light. Some observers believe that some WTO members may reevaluate the basis for their opposition to some version of the agreement proposed in July 2008 based on today's radically different economic environment. This is, in part, due to the fact that shrinking trade flows have highlighted the importance of open markets for economic development among a broad group of countries, and in the process, increased the value of concessions left on the negotiating table last year. This group includes the export-dependent countries in Asia countries and India. Other observers think that the kind of political leadership that is necessary to push trade liberalization will be in short supply and difficult to secure in a time of a global recession and increased protectionist pressures. Moreover, the U.S. business community is not enthusiastic about the package of market opening concessions that was proposed last July, thus providing little stakeholder support in the United States for an effort to reach a partial Doha agreement.

End Notes

[1] *International Monetary Fund,* IMF Survey Online, March 19, 2009.

[2] Alan Beattie, "Policymakers Strive to Explain Plunge in Trade," *Financial Times,* March 9. 2009.

[3] See Carter Dougherty, "Protectionism: The View from Europe," *New York Times,* March 9, 2009; Catherine Rampell, "The Contagion of Protectionism," *New York Times,* March 6, 2009; Anthony Faiola, "Trade Barriers Threaten Global Economy: World Bank Finds Protectionist Trend," *Washington Post,* March 18, 2009; Jeffrey E. Garten, "The Dangers of Turning Inward," *The Wall Street Journal,* March 1, 2009; and Ariana Eunjung Cha, "U.S.-China Trade Ties Erode Amid Accusations From Each Nation Complaining of Protectionism," *Washington Post,* February 20, 2009.

[4] Some 26 WTO members, including Australia, Brazil, India, and South Korea, impose tariffs (so-called "applied" tariffs) that average roughly 8 percent. Because these tariffs have not been "bound" through WTO negotiations, they could be raised as high as 28 percent on average without breaking any WTO rules or requirement to compensate affected trade partners. The potential costs if these countries decided to increase tariff rates to their bound level to protect domestic industries are potentially significant, decreasing world trade by an estimated 7.7 percent. See Antoine Bouet and David Laborde, "The Potential Cost of A Failed Doha Round," *International Food Policy Research Institute,,* Issue Brief 56, December 2008.

[5] Paul Blustein, "The Nine-Day Misadventure of the Most Favored Nations: How the WTO's Doha Round Negotiations Went Awry in July, 2008," *Brookings Institution,* 2009.

[6] The simple average share of world trade to GDP, which is 96% today compared to 70% in 1970, illustrates the increased interdependence. Source: World Bank.

[7] Dick K. Nanto, *Globalized Supply Chains and U.S. Policy,* CRS Report R40 167, *Globalized Supply Chains and U.S. Policy*, by Dick K. Nanto, January 16, 2009.

[8] Douglas A. Irwin, "Trade Policy in 2008: Great Depression Redux?", In *What World Leaders Must Do to Halt the Spread of Protectionism,* Richard Baldwin and Simon Evenett, editors, A VoxEU.org Publication, Centre for Economic Policy Research (CEPR) 2008, p. 61.

[9] Wendy Dobson, "Keeping the Global Economy Open," In Richard Baldwin and Simon Evenett, p. 28.

[10] There are wide variations among countries between agricultural and manufactured goods.

[11] WTO Staff, "Report to the TPRB From the Director-General on the Financial and Economic Crisis and Trade- Related Developments," JOB(09)2, January 23, 2009.

[12] Bureau of National Affairs, "WTO Report Finds Limited Impact So Far Of Financial Crisis on Higher Trade Barriers," *International Trade Reporter,* January 27, 2009.

[13] Elisa Gamberoni and Richard Newfarmer, "Trade Protection: Incipient but Worrisome Trends," *World Bank,* VOX, March 4, 2009.

[14] The provision provides that none of the funds appropriated or otherwise made available by the act may be used for a project for the construction, alteration, maintenance, or repair of a public building or public work unless all of the iron, steel, and manufactured goods used in the project are produced in the Unites States provided such action would not be inconsistent with the public interest, such products are not produced in the United States, and would not increase the cost of the overall project by more than 25%. U.S. major trading partners have similar buy domestic provisions.

[15] Louis Uchitelle, "Buy America' in Stimulus (but Good Luck With That)," *New York Times,* February 21, 2009. Much of the actual impact will depend on how the various federal agencies interpret and administer the provision. In the past, U.S. agencies have shown flexibility in interpreting specific definitions and vague language in a way that has been consistent with U.S. international trade obligations.

[16] Buy American provisions, in different forms, have been a significant response to the belief that U.S. products and materials in some circumstances should be protected to some degree from foreign competition in order to obtain the biggest bang for the buck from federal spending. Critics respond that federal spending would yield the biggest bang for the buck by sourcing inputs and goods internationally.

[17] *The Economist,* "The Next Great Wall: Buy Local Campaigns Raise Protectionist Barriers in Asia," March 14, 2009.

[18] Ben Hall and Peggy Holinger, "France Opts for 6 Billion Euro Car Bail-Out," *Financial Times,* February 10, 2009.

[19] Niki Tait, "Brussels and France Resolve Auto Dispute," *Financial Times,* March 2, 2009.

[20] Elisa Gamberoni and Richard Newfarmer, p. 3.

[21] Simon J. Evenett and Frederic Jenny, "Bailouts: How to Discourage a Subsidies War," In Richard Baldwin and Simon Evenett, *The Collapse of Global Trade: Murky Protectionism and the Crisis: Recommendations for the G20,* A VoxEU.org Publication, Centre for Economic Policy Research (CEPR), 2009.

[22] *Inside U.S. Trade,* "Possible U.S. Auto Bailout Could Face WTO Challenge By EU," November 21, 2008.

[23] *Inside U.S. Trade,* "Experts Say Auto Bailout Provides Illegal WTO Benefit, Risking Trade," December 26, 2006

[24] CVD laws are designed to offset to any unfair competitive advantage that foreign manufacturers or exporters may enjoy over domestic producers as a result of foreign countervailable subsidies.

[25] This challenge would have to be heard domestically and would not constitute tit for tat retaliation.

[26] Claire Brunel and Gary Hufbauer, "Money for the Auto Industry: Consistent with WTO Rules," *Peterson Institute for International Economics,* Number PB09-4, February 2009, p. 10.

[27] Simon J. Evenett and Frederic Jenny, p. 84.

[28] Claire Brunel and Gary Hufbauer, pp 9-10.

[29] Landon Thomas, Jr., "Nationalized in All But Name: U.S. Move Echoes U.K. Share of RBS," *International Herald Tribune,* February 24, 2009, Internet edition.

[30] Binyamin Appelbaum, "Government to Take Bigger Stake in Citigroup," *Washington Post,* February 27, 2009.

[31] Anthony Faiola, "Out of Gaps in Treaties, First Salvos of Trade War," *Washington Post,* January 1, 2009.

[32] The current account is the broadest measure of a country's international transactions and includes trade in goods, services, investments, and unilateral transfers. A surplus means that outflows of currency resulting from these transactions are less than inflows, and a deficit means that outflows of currency resulting from these transactions exceed inflows. Thus, a current account surplus country is a net exporter of investment funds to the rest of the world, and a current account deficit country is a net importer or recipient of investment funds from the rest of the world.

[33] The oil exporters generated $813 billion, China $399 billion or 9.5% of GDP, Germany $279 billion or 7.3% of GDP, and Japan $194 billion or 4% of GDP. Cited in Martin Wolf, "Global Imbalances threaten the survival of liberal trade," *Financial Times,* December 2, 2008.

[34] CRS Report RL34742, *The Global Financial and Economic Crisis: Analysis and Policy Implications,* by Dick K. Nanto, James K. Jackson, Wayne M. Morison, J. Michael Donnelly, Martin A. Weiss, Ben Dolven, William H. Cooper, J. F. Hornbeck, February 20, 2009.

[35] U.S. Joint Economic Committee, "Chinese FX Interventions Caused International Imbalances, Contributed to U.S. Housing Bubble," by Robert O'Quinn, March 2008.

[36] Robert Samuelson, "Three Crises in One," *Washington Post,* January 26, 2009.

[37] The other large current account deficit countries in descending order are Spain, the United Kingdom, France, Italy, and Australia.

[38] In the short-run, U.S. policy is attempting to boost spending and reduce savings in order to soften the downturn, which paradoxically makes the goal of rebalancing more difficult in the long-run.

[39] William R. Cline, "Trade, Finance, and the Global Recession," p.8, and CRS Report RL33577, *U.S. International Trade: Trends and Forecasts, U.S. International Trade: Trends and Forecasts,* By Dick K. Nanto, Shayerah Ilias, and J. Michael Donnelly, p.27.

[40] William R. Cline, and Martin Wolf, "Why Obama Must Mend A World Economy," *Financial Times,* January 20, 2009.

[41] The stimulus package, of course, is controversial in the United States.

[42] Landon Thomas Jr. and Julia Werdigier, "No Clear Accord on Stimulus By Top 20 Industrial Nations," *New York Times,* March 15, 2009.

[43] For an critical analysis suggesting that China's stimulus program will do little to stimulate imports and domestic consumption, see Derek Scissors, "China's Stimulus Plan: Repackaged and Misdirected," *Heritage Foundation,* Web Memo #2 128, November 10, 2008.

[44] Martin Wolf, "Global Imbalances Threaten the Survival of Liberal Trade," *Financial Times, December 2, 2008.*

[45] To date this has not happened as global investors continue to buy U.S. bonds, strengthening, rather than weakening, the value of the dollar. See Peter S. Goodman, "A Rising Dollar Lifts the U.S. but Adds to the Crisis Abroad," *New York Times,* March 9, 2009.

[46] Michael Pettis, "Would A Trade War Solve the Problem of Excess Capacity," *Emerging Capital Markets Economic Monitor,* November 17, 2008.

[47] Martin Wolf, "Why Saving the World Economy Should Be Affordable," *Financial Times,* March 18. 2009.

[48] Keith Bradsher, "As Trade Slows, China Rethinks Its Growth Strategy," *New York Times,* January 1, 2009, and Steven Pearlstein, "Asia, Europe Find Their Supply Chains Yanked, Beware the Backlash," *Washington Post,* February 20, 2009.

[49] David Pilling, "Japan's New Carry Trade, The Handbag," *Financial Times,* January 22, 2009.

[50] Carter Dougherty and Judy Dempsey, "Leary of Debt, Germany Shuns a Spending Spree," *Financial Times,* March 10, 2009.

[51] Keith Bradsher, "As Trade Slows, China Rethinks its Growth Strategy," *New York Times,* January 9, 2009.

[52] Edward Cody, "E.U. Pushes Strict Regulations Over More Stimulus Spending," *Washington Post,* March 21, 2009.

[53] The IMF analysis relies on the size of a country's output gap and the amount of "fiscal space" as determined by levels of deficits, public debt, and interest rates as key determinants of the magnitude of a country's overall fiscal expansion. See IMF Staff Analysis, pp. 3-4.

[54] Alan Beattie, "IMF Firepower to Triple," *Financial Times,* March 12, 2009.

[55] C. Fred Bergsten, "Needed: A Global Response to the Global Economic and Financial Crisis," Testimony before the Subcommittee on Terrorism, Nonproliferation and Trade, Committee on Foreign Affairs, U.S. House of Representatives, March 12, 2009.

[56] Martin Wolf, "What Obama Should Tell the Leaders of the Group of 20," *Financial Times,* February 25, 2009.

[57] Richard Baldwin, "The Crisis and Protectionism: History Doesn't Repeat Itself, But Sometimes It Rhymes," In Richard Baldwin and Simon Evenett, p. 33.

[58] Kevin H. O'Rourke, "Engage Multilateral Institutions In Solutions To Today's Problems," In Richard Baldwin and Simon Everett, p. 56.

[59] Raymond J. Ahearn and Alfred Reifman, "U.S. Trade Policy: Congress Sends A Message," In Current U.S. Trade Policy: Analysis, Agenda, and Administration, *NBER Conference Report,* Robert E. Baldwin and J. David Richardson, editors, 1986.

[60] Michael Pettis, "This Is Not the Time to Attack China," *Financial Times,* February 18, 2009.

[61] It may be hard for the United States to induce China to appreciate its currency while inducing it also to buy U.S. debt since China's undervalued currency is the chief reason why China has to buy that debt.

In: U.S. Trade, Protectionism and the Global... ISBN: 978-1-60876-966-7
Editors: Andrew J. Caldwell

Chapter 3

U.S. International Trade: Trends and Forecasts

Dick K. Nanto, Shayerah Ilias and Michael J. Donnelly

Summary

The U.S. trade deficit is shrinking primarily because the global financial crisis is causing U.S. imports to drop faster than U.S. exports. The global simultaneous recession, however, implies that exporting countries cannot rely on increased foreign demand to make up for slack demand at home. Even though U.S. imports are projected to decline, companies competing with imports are still likely to face diminishing demand as the domestic economy shrinks. These conditions imply that the political forces to protect domestic industry from imports are likely to intensify both in the United States and abroad.

In 2008, the trade deficit in goods reached $821.2 billion on a balance of payments (BoP) basis, up slightly from $819.4 billion in 2007 but less than the $838.3 billion in 2006. The 2008 deficit on merchandise trade with China was $266.3 billion (Census basis), with the European Union was $93.4 billion, with Japan was $72.7 billion, with Canada was $74.2 billion, with Mexico was $64.4 billion, and the Asian Newly Industrialized Countries (Hong Kong, South Korea, Singapore, and Taiwan) was $3.8 billion. Imports of goods of $2,112.5 billion increased by $144.7 billion (7.3%) over 2007. Exports of goods of $1,291.3 billion rose by $142.8 billion (12.4%). Although the overall trade deficit for 2008 was up, in the fourth quarter as the U.S. recession worsened, imports declined faster than exports resulting in a trade deficit for the month of December that was $23.0 billion less than the comparable deficit for July.

Trade deficits are a concern for Congress because they may generate trade friction and pressures for the government to do more to open foreign markets, to shield U.S. producers from foreign competition, or to assist U.S. industries to become more competitive. Overall U.S. trade deficits reflect excess spending (a shortage of savings) in the domestic economy and a reliance on capital imports to finance that shortfall. Capital inflows serve to offset the outflow of dollars used to pay for imports. Movements in the exchange rate help to balance trade. The rising trade deficit (when not matched by capital inflows) places downward pressure on the value of the dollar which, in turn, helps to shrink the deficit by making U.S. exports cheaper and imports more expensive. Central banks in countries such as China, however, have intervened in foreign exchange markets to keep the value of their currencies from rising too fast.

The broadest measure of U.S. international economic transactions is the balance on current account. In addition to merchandise trade, it includes trade in services and unilateral transfers. In 2007, the deficit on current account fell to a revised $738.6 billion from a revised $811.5 billion in 2006. In trade in advanced technology products, the U.S. balance improved from a deficit of $38 billion in 2006 but deteriorated to $53 billion in 2007 and $56 billion in 2008. In trade in motor vehicles and parts, the $107 billion U.S. deficit in 2007 was mainly with Japan, Mexico, Germany, and South Korea. In crude oil, major sources of the $342 billion in imports were Canada, Saudi Arabia, Venezuela, Nigeria, and Mexico. This report will be updated periodically.

Most Recent Developments

As the global financial crisis has worsened and the United States and other countries drop into recession, the declining U.S. trade deficit is likely to contribute positively to U.S. gross domestic product. The U.S. recession would be worse without the shrinking U.S. trade deficit. In 2009, world economic growth is projected to be less than 1% or even negative, and North America, Japan, and Europe are experiencing a simultaneous recession.

These recessionary economic conditions have combined with trillions of dollars lost in equity markets and a credit squeeze that is threatening the health of numerous businesses all over the world. A major problem is that exporting countries cannot rely on increased foreign demand to make up for slack demand at home. There is little prospect that they can export their way out of this recession. Even though U.S. imports are projected to decline, companies competing with imports are still likely to face diminishing demand as the domestic economy shrinks. These conditions imply that the political forces to protect domestic industry from imports are likely to intensify both in the United States and abroad.

In 2009, the U.S. deficit in merchandise trade is projected to drop by about half (relative to 2008) to around $435 billion as the U.S. recession causes imports to decline faster than exports. Total U.S. trade (exports plus imports of goods and services) also is projected to fall by about 21%.

In 2009, imports of petroleum and products are projected to fall by about 60% as moderating prices for crude oil and weakening domestic demand for gasoline and other petroleum products cut into the need for imports.

Trade in Goods

In 2008, the trade deficit in goods reached $821.2 billion on a balance of payments (BoP) basis, up slightly from $819.4 billion in 2007 but less than the $838.3 billion in 2006. The 2008 deficit on merchandise trade with China was $266.3 billion (Census basis), with the European Union was $93.4 billion, with Japan was $72.7 billion, with Canada was $74.2 billion, with Mexico was $64.4 billion, and the Asian Newly Industrialized Countries (Hong Kong, South Korea, Singapore, and Taiwan) was $3.8 billion. Imports of goods of $2,112.5 billion increased by $144.7 billion (7.3%) over 2007. Increases in imports by sector were: crude oil up $104.8 billion, capital goods except automotive up $9.2 billion, automotive vehicles and parts down $25.2 billion, and consumer goods up $7.6 billion. Exports of goods of $1,291.3 billion rose by $142.8 billion (12.4%), particularly in industrial supplies, up $70.9 billion, capital goods except automotive up $22.0 billion, automotive vehicles and parts down $0.1 billion, and consumer goods up $15.1 billion. Although the overall trade deficit was up, in the fourth quarter as the U.S. recession worsened, imports declined faster than exports resulting in a small quarterly trade deficit. U.S. exports and imports of goods began to decline in August 2008. In December 2008, exports of goods were $32.0 billion lower and imports were $55.1 billion lower than in July 2008. This resulted in a trade deficit for the month of December that was $23.0 billion less than the comparable deficit for July.

Trade in Services

In 2008, total annual imports of services of $407.6 billion and exports of $551.6 billion yielded a surplus in U.S. services trade of $144.0 billion. The U.S. service industries, particularly, financial services, tourism, shipping, and insurance, tend to compete well in international markets. In August 2008, U.S. services exports and imports peaked and have declined slightly each month since.

Trade in Goods and Services

Since the United States runs a surplus in trade in services, the combined deficit on goods and services is lower than the deficit on goods alone. In 2008, exports of goods and services of $1,843.0 and imports of $2,520.1 resulted in a deficit of $677.1 billion, down from the $700.3 billion in 2007 and the $753.3 billion in 2006.

For 2008, the annual trade deficit on goods and services amounted to approximately 4.7% of U.S. gross domestic product (GDP, $14.3 trillion in 2008), down slightly from 5.1% in 2007 and 5.4% in 2006. A level of 5% for countries is considered to be cautionary by economic observers. At that level, other countries have experienced problems paying for imports and maintaining the value of their currency. Given the "safe haven" effect (investors seeking a safe investment) for U.S. Treasury securities, however, as the global financial crisis has worsened, foreign investors have flocked to U.S. securities. As a result, U.S. interest rates have remained relatively low, and in combination with the declining U.S. trade deficit have worked to allay concerns over the ability of the United States to finance the excess of imports over exports.

This report provides an overview of the current status, trends, and forecasts for U.S. import and export flows as well as certain balances. The purpose of this report is to provide current data and brief explanations for the various types of trade flows along with a brief discussion of trends that may require attention or point to the need for policy changes.

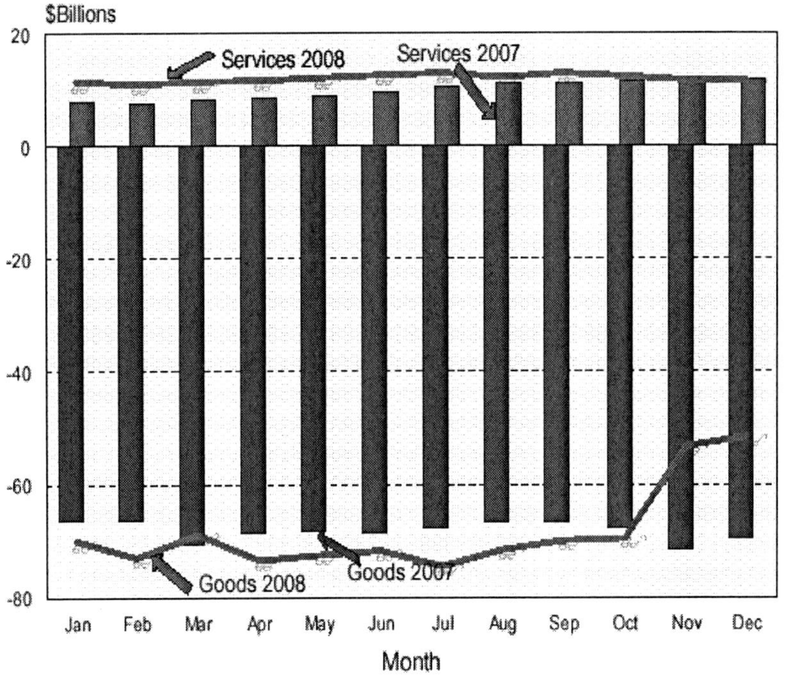

Source: CRS with Data from the U.S. Department of Commerce.

Figure 1. Monthly U.S. Balances of Trade in Goods and Services, 2007 and 2008 (in Current Dollars)

Figure 1 shows U.S. trade balances in goods and services by month. 2007 data is graphed in bars; 2008 data is graphed in lines. In 2007, the monthly surplus in services gradually rose from $7.8 billion to $11.9 billion. The 2008 monthly services balance averages close to $12 billion. Total 2008 annual imports of services of $407.6 billion and exports of $551.6 billion yielded a surplus in U.S. services trade of $144.0 billion.[1] The December 2008 monthly deficit on goods and services of $40.0 was the lowest monthly deficit in three years.

The use of trade policy as an economic or strategic tool is beyond the scope of this report but can be found in various other CRS reports.[2] Further detail on trade in specific commodities, with particular countries or regions, or for different time periods, can be obtained from the Department of Commerce,[3] U.S. International Trade Commission,[4] or by contacting the authors of this report.

The U.S. Deficit in International Trade

International trade in goods and services along with flows of financial capital affect virtually every person living in the United States. Whether buying imported clothes, gasoline, computers or cars, or working in an industry that competes with imports, or sells products abroad, the influence of international trade on economic activity is ubiquitous. Although the United States is one of the three largest exporters in the world (China and Germany are the other two), U.S. sales abroad are overshadowed by the huge demand by Americans for imported products. Since 1976, the United States has incurred continual merchandise trade deficits with annual amounts increasing steadily until the past two years.

For the Congress, the trade deficit and other aspects of international trade enter into public policy considerations through many portals. At the macroeconomic level, trade deficits are a concern because they affect U.S. economic growth, interest rates, labor, and the debt load of the economy. As the trade deficit rises relative to the total economy, the risk increases that the dollar will weaken, raise prices, disrupt financial markets, and reduce the economic well being of the population. On the strategic level, trade ties often lead to a deepening of bilateral relations with other nations that can develop into formal free trade agreements or political and security arrangements. Trade also can be used as a tool to accomplish strategic objectives—particularly through providing preferential trading arrangements or by imposing trade sanctions.

In the current financial crisis, countries may turn inward to rescue their own businesses and economies even if such actions come at the expense of the international benefit. By necessity, this may involve seeking national advantage by either protecting domestic industries or promoting exports.

On the microeconomic side, imports of specific products can generate trade friction and pressures from constituent interests for the government to shield U.S. producers from foreign competition, provide adjustment assistance, open foreign markets, or assist U.S. industries to become more competitive.

Savings Shortfalls and the Trade Deficit

Overall U.S. trade deficits reflect a shortage of savings in the domestic economy and a reliance on capital imports to finance that shortfall. A savings shortfall is the analogue of excessive spending that is financed by borrowing. Households borrow for consumption; businesses borrow to invest; and the government borrows to cover its budget deficit. At the international transaction level, the savings shortfall is manifest when the United States imports capital to pay for its excess of imports (trade deficit).

Whether this foreign borrowing is beneficial for the U.S. economy depends on how the imports of capital are used. If they are used to finance investments that generate a future return at a sufficiently high rate (they raise future output and productivity), then they may increase the well- being of current and future generations. However, if the imports are used only for current consumption, the net effect of the borrowing will be to shift the burden of repayment to future generations without a corresponding benefit to them.

Implications of the Trade Deficit

U.S. trade balances are macroeconomic variables that may or may not indicate underlying problems with the competitiveness of particular industries or what some refer to as the competitiveness of a nation. The reason is that overall trade flows are determined, within the framework of institutional barriers to trade and the activities of individual industries, primarily by macroeconomic factors such as rates of growth, savings and investment behavior (including government budget deficits/surpluses), international capital flows, and exchange rates.[5]

Increases in trade deficits may diminish economic growth, since net exports (exports minus imports) are a component of gross domestic product. In the late 1980s and early 1990s, export growth was an important element in overall U.S. economic growth. In 2006, merchandise exports accounted for about 7.7% of GDP, compared with 5.9% in 1990. Recently, however, rising trade deficits have reduced total domestic demand in the economy, but the weakness in the trade sector has been offset by strong consumer, business, and government demand.

Many economists fear that the rising U.S. trade and current account[6] deficits could lead to a large drop in the value of the U.S. dollar. The current account deficit, while decreasing from 6.2% of GDP in 2006 to 5.1% of GDP in 2007, continues to place downward pressure on the dollar. A weakened dollar boosts exports by making them cheaper, narrowing the U.S. trade deficit. Compared to a Federal Reserve index of major currencies weighted by importance to U.S. trade, the dollar has lost a third of its value since 2002 (see

Figure 2). The dollar has fallen against the euro, yen, British pound, Australian dollar, and Canadian dollar. In fact, the U.S. dollar fell to parity with the Canadian loonie in September 2007 for the first time in thirty years, and remains roughly in that range. Between July and November 2008, the U.S. dollar strengthened against other currencies as the global financial crisis increased "safe haven demand" for the dollar. Since November, the dollar has lost some value, partly due to the Federal Reserve's lowering of interest rates.

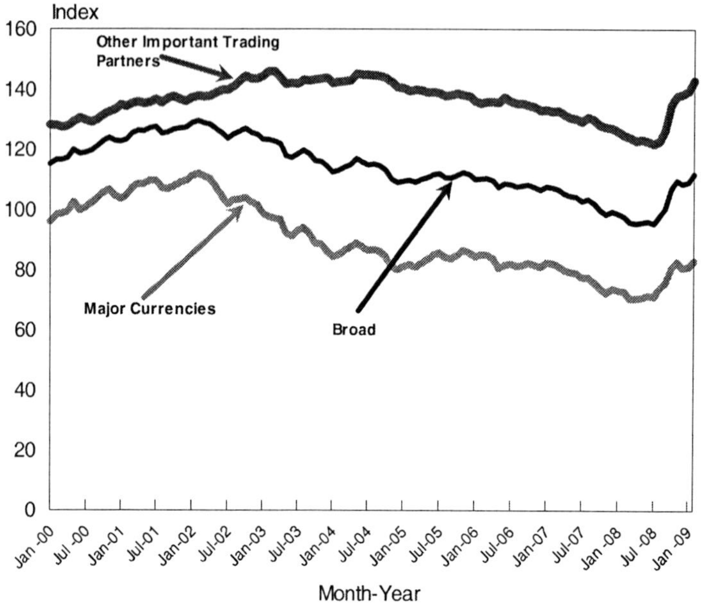

Source: Federal Reserve Bank of St. Louis, http://research.stlouisfed.org/.

Notes: Broad Index (January 1997 = 100): Euro Area, Canada, Japan, Mexico, China, United Kingdom, Taiwan, Korea, Singapore, Hong Kong, Malaysia, Brazil, Switzerland, Thailand, Philippines, Australia, Indonesia, India, Israel, Saudi Arabia, Russia, Sweden, Argentina, Venezuela, Chile and Colombia.

Major Currencies Index (January 1973 = 100): Euro Area, Canada, Japan, United Kingdom, Switzerland, Australia, and Sweden.

Other Important Trade Partners Index (January 1997 = 100): Mexico, China, Taiwan, Korea, Singapore, Hong Kong, Malaysia, Brazil, Thailand, Philippines, Indonesia, India, Israel, Saudi Arabia, Russia, Argentina, Venezuela, Chile and Colombia.

Figure 2. Month-End Trade-Weighted U.S. Dollar Against Broad, Major Currencies, and Other Important Trading Partner Indices, January 2000-October 2008

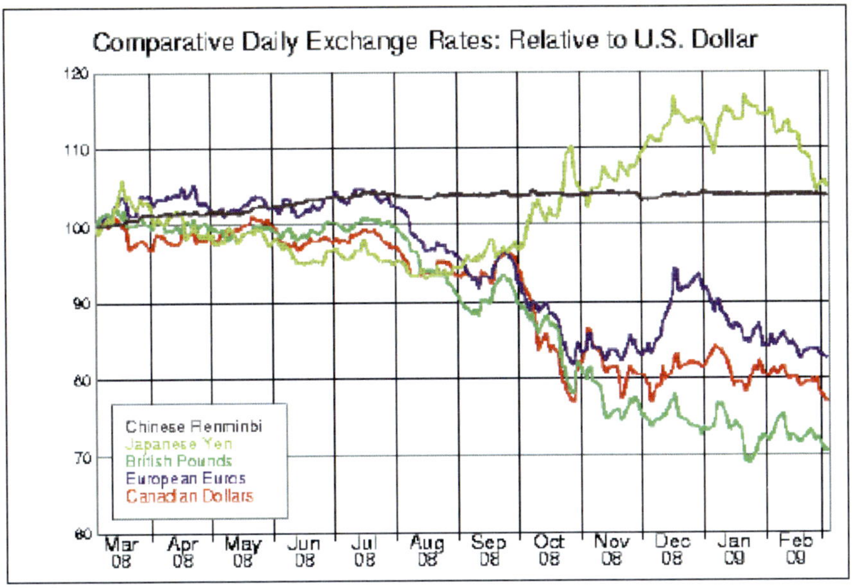

Source: Werner Antweiler, University of British Columbia, Vancouver BC, Canada. PACIFIC Exchange Rate Service

Figure 3. The Exchange Value of the Chinese Renminbi, Japanese Yen, British Pound, EU Euro, and Canadian Dollar

Although a weakened dollar helps to reduce U.S. trade imbalances, it also may reduce the dollar's attractiveness to foreign investors. If foreign investors stop offsetting the deficit by buying dollar- denominated assets, the value of the dollar could drop—possibly precipitously. In that case, U.S. interest rates would have to rise to attract more foreign investment; financial markets could be disrupted; and inflationary pressures could increase. The global financial crisis has worked to strengthen the dollar vis-a-vis the EU euro, UK pound, Canadian dollar, and many currencies of developing nations. The Japanese yen has appreciated considerably but recently has been depreciating relative to the dollar. The Chinese renminbi appreciated somewhat until mid-2008, but since then has been steady.

Currently, foreign investment in dollar assets along with purchases of securities by investors seeking a safe haven as well as from central banks of countries such as China have bolstered the value of the dollar. China's central bank has intervened in currency markets to keep its exchange rate relatively stable. Japan claims not to have intervened in currency markets since spring of 2004. This intervention adds to the foreign currency reserves held by these countries. As of the end of December 2008, Japan's central bank held $982 billion in foreign currency reserves,[7] and the Bank of China held $1,946 billion.[8] In U.S. Treasury securities, as of December 2008, Japan held $626 billion and China $727 billion.[9] On July 21, 2005, China announced a 2.1% revaluation of its currency, and the value of the renminbi has appreciated steadily from 8.2 to 7.0 renminbi per dollar (15%). Continuing in that range, on February 4, 2008, the renminbi was trading at 5.3 per dollar.

A recent development in foreign country holdings of dollars and other reserve currencies is that some are turning toward creating sovereign wealth funds (SWFs). These are funds owned by governments that are invested in stocks, bonds, property, and other financial instruments denominated in dollars, euros, or other hard currency. For China, Japan, South Korea, Russia, and the oil-exporting nations of the Persian Gulf, the source of capital for these funds is coming from governmental holdings of foreign exchange. For China and Japan, for example, foreign exchange reserves have traditionally been invested by their respective central banks primarily in low- yielding but low-risk government bonds, i.e., U.S. Treasury securities. The purpose of sovereign wealth funds is to diversify investments and to earn a higher rate of return. For example, in September 2007, China created a sovereign wealth fund—the China Investment Corporation (CIC)—with initial capital of $200 billion. Depending on how these funds are managed and what leverage they acquire, they could affect U.S. interest rates (foreign purchases of U.S. Treasury securities tend to reduce U.S. interest rates), corporate activities (if funds buy significant voting shares of companies), and foreign access to technology and raw materials. The U.S. trade deficit provides some of the foreign exchange that goes to finance these sovereign wealth funds.[10]

How long can the United States keep running trade deficits? U.S. deficits in trade can continue for as long as foreign investors are willing to buy and hold U.S. assets, particularly government securities and other financial assets.[11] Their willingness depends on a complicated array of factors including the perception of the United States as a safe haven for capital, relative rates of return on investments, interest rates on U.S. financial assets, actions by foreign central banks, and the savings and investment decisions of businesses, governments, and households. The policy levers that influence these factors that affect the trade deficit are held by the Federal Reserve[12] (interest rates) as well as both Congress and the Administration (government budget deficits and trade policy), and their counterpart institutions abroad.

In the 111th Congress, legislation directed at the trade deficit has been taking several strategies. Some address trade barriers by particular countries, particularly China. Others are aimed at preventing manipulation of exchange rates or at imposing import duties to compensate for the arguably undervalued Chinese currency.[13] Other bills seek to find domestic substitutes for imported oil, or require the President or a policy group to take certain actions if the trade deficit exceeded a threshold amount. Legislation is tracked in other CRS reports dealing with trade.

Types of Trade Data

The U.S. government compiles trade data in four different ways. The data on goods trade are first compiled on a Census basis. Bilateral and sectoral data are reported only on a Census basis. The Census numbers are then adjusted and reported monthly on a balance of payments (BoP) basis that includes adjustments for valuation, coverage, and timing and excludes military transactions. The data are finally reported in terms of national income and product accounts (NIPA). The NIPA data also can be further adjusted to include correcting for inflation to gauge movement in trade volumes as distinct from trade values. Conceptually, this procedure is analogous to adjusting macroeconomic data from nominal to real values.

The Census Bureau also reports imports on a c.i.f. (cost, insurance, and freight) basis which includes the value of insurance, international shipping, and other charges incurred in bringing merchandise to U.S. ports of entry. The customs (or f.a.s.—free alongside ship) data do not include these supplementary costs. U.S. import data are reported on a customs basis with insurance and freight charges counted in U.S. services trade. Other countries, however, commonly report merchandise import figures that include insurance and freight charges. This tends to overstate their imports and understate their trade surpluses with the United States.

U.S. Merchandise Trade Balance

The merchandise (goods) trade balance is the most widely known and frequently used indicator of U.S. international economic activity (see **Figure 4**). In 2008, total U.S. merchandise trade amounted to $3,404 billion, an 8.4% increase from $3,116 billion in 2007. Merchandise exports in 2008 totaled $1,291 billion, while imports reached $2,112 billion (BoP basis). The U.S.

merchandise trade deficit rose slightly from $819 billion in 2007 to $821 billion in 2008 after dropping slightly in 2007. Prior to this, the merchandise deficit increased in double-digit rates by 22% in 2004 and 18% in 2005. The deficit increase slowed in 2006, increasing by only 6.5%.

U.S. merchandise exports (as shown in Table 1 and Figure 5), decreased in 2001 and 2002 in response to the global slowdown, but generally have been increasing each year. As shown in Figure 5, the growth of imports has also been steady, although they too fell by 6.4% in 2001 before recovering in 2002. In 2003, import growth was nearly double export growth, although in 2004, export growth almost caught up with that of imports, and in 2005, the rate of increase for both dropped slightly. Growth in exports and imports slowed in 2007 with exports rising by 12.3% and imports by 5.7%. Likewise in 2008, exports grew faster than imports (12.4% vs 7.3%), but the trade deficit still increased. This is because U.S. imports are about 63% greater than U.S. exports, so exports must grow about 63% faster than imports just for the deficit to remain constant.

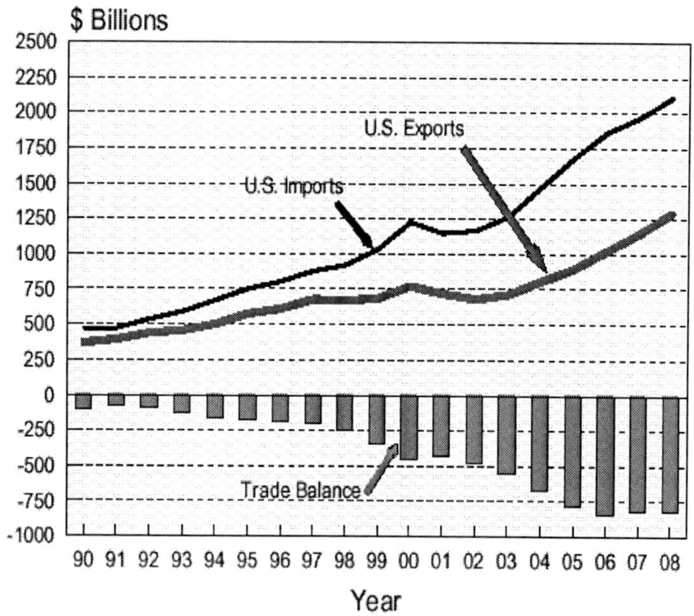

Source: CRS with data from U.S. Bureau of Economic Analysis http://www.bea.gov/, IMF

Figure 4. U.S. Merchandise Exports, Imports, and Trade Balance

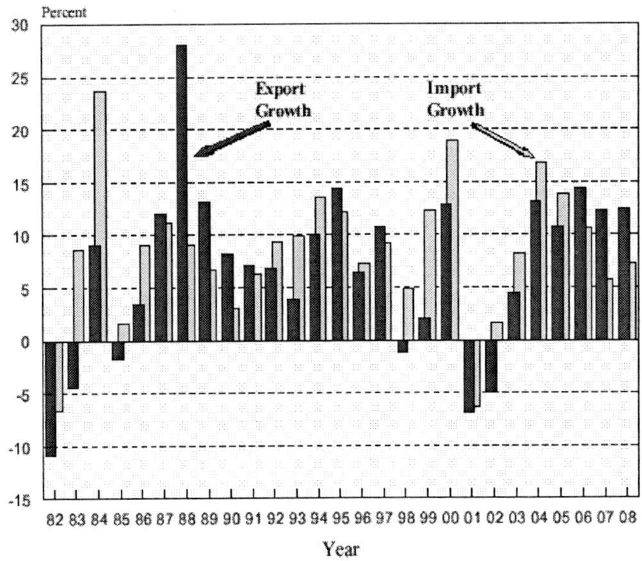

Source: Underlying data from U.S. Department of Commerce.

Figure 5. Annual Growth in U.S. Merchandise Exports and Imports, 1982-2007

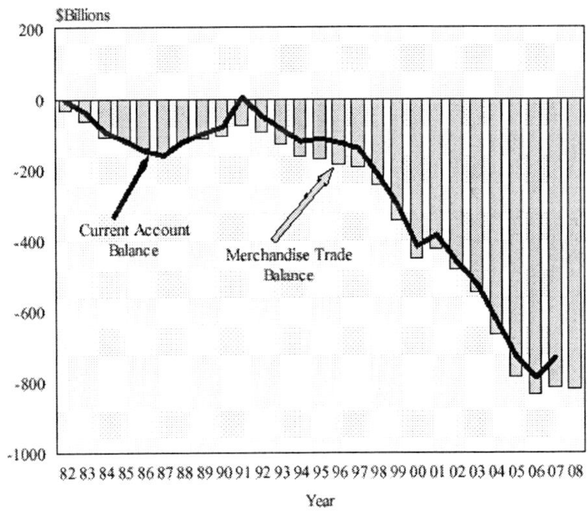

Source: CRS with data from U.S. Bureau of Economic Analysis, U.S. International Transactions Account.

Figure 6. U.S. Current Account and Merchandise Trade Balances

CURRENT ACCOUNT BALANCE

The current account provides a broader measure of U.S. trade because it includes services, investment income, and unilateral transfers in addition to merchandise trade (see). The balance on services includes travel, transportation, fees and royalties, insurance payments, and other government and private services. The balance on investment income includes income received on U.S. assets abroad minus income paid on foreign assets in the United States. Unilateral transfers are international transfers of funds for which there is no *quid pro quo*. These include private gifts, remittances, pension payments, and government grants (foreign aid). Data on the current account are announced several months later than those on trade in goods and services.

Table 2 summarizes the components of the U.S. current account. In 2007, the U.S. deficit on current account decreased to $731.2 from $788.1 in 2006. The 2007 deficit on current account amounted to 5.3 % of GDP. This remains above the caution level used by the International Monetary Fund of 5%. Since the dollar is used as an international reserve currency, however, the United States can run trade deficits without the same downward pressure on the value of the dollar as other nations. Historically, the current account deficit fell from a then record-high $160.7 billion in 1987 to $79.0 billion in 1990, and switched to a $3.7 billion surplus in 1991 (primarily because of payments to fund the Gulf War by Japan and other nations). However, since a slight decline in 1995, the current account deficit has been increasing significantly except for a slight dip in 2001 because of the U.S. recession and a similar situation in 2007.

Because the merchandise trade balance comprises the greater part of the current account, the two tend to track each other. Unlike the merchandise trade balance, however, the services account registered a $85.0 billion surplus in 2006 and $119.1 billion surplus in 2007. Since Americans are such large investors in foreign economies, the United States traditionally also has a surplus in its investment income ($81.7 billion in 2007), but the deficit in unilateral transfers (primarily dollars sent abroad by foreign workers and recent immigrants) totaled $92.0 billion in 2006 and $112.7 billion in 2007. Unilateral transfers have now reached more than triple the level of the late 1980s.

Table 1. U.S. Exports, Imports, and Merchandise Trade Balances (billions of U.S. dollars)

Year	Census basis			Balance of payments basis		
	Exports (f.a.s.)[a]	Imports (customs)[b]	Trade Balance	Exports (f.a.s.)[a]	Imports (customs)[b]	Trade Balance
1982	212.3	243.9	-31.6	211.2	247.6	-36.4
1983	201.7	261.7	-60.0	201.8	268.9	-67.1
1984	218.7	330.5	-111.8	219.9	332.4	-112.5
1985	212.6	336.4	-123.8	215.9	338.1	-122.2
1986	226.4	365.7	-139.3	223.3	368.4	-145.1
1987	253.9	406.3	-152.4	250.2	409.8	-159.6
1988	323.3	441.9	-118.6	320.2	447.2	-127.0
1989	362.9	473.4	-110.5	359.9	477.7	-117.8
1990	392.9	495.2	-102.3	387.4	498.4	-111.0
1991	421.8	487.1	-65.3	414.1	491.0	-76.9
1992	448.2	532.6	-84.4	439.6	536.5	-96.9
1993	464.8	580.5	-115.7	456.9	589.4	-132.5
1994	512.6	663.2	-150.6	502.9	668.7	-165.8
1995	584.7	743.5	-158.8	575.2	749.4	-174.2
1996	625.1	795.3	-170.2	612.1	803.1	-191.0
1997	689.2	869.7	-180.5	678.4	876.8	-198.4
1998	682.1	911.9	-229.8	670.4	918.6	-248.2
1999	695.8	1,024.6	-328.8	684.0	1031.8	-347.8
2000	781.9	1,218.0	-436.1	772.0	1226.7	-454.7
2001	730.9	1,142.3	-411.4	718.7	1148.2	-429.5
2002	693.5	1,163.6	-470.1	682.4	1167.4	-485.0
2003	724.8	1,257.1	-532.3	713.4	1264.3	-550.9
2004	818.8	1,469.7	-650.9	807.5	1477.1	-669.6
2005	906.0	1,673.5	-767.5	894.6	1681.8	-787.1
2006	1,036.6	1,853.9	-817.3	1023.1	1861.4	-838.3
2007	1,162.5	1,957.0	-794.5	1148.5	1967.9	-819.4
2008	1,300.5	2,100.4	-799.9	1291.3	2112.5	-821.2

Source: U.S. Department of Commerce, Bureau of Economic Analysis, U.S. International Transactions Accounts Data.

Note: Goods on a Census basis are adjusted to a BoP basis to include changes in ownership that occur without goods passing into or out of the customs territory of the United States, to eliminate duplication, and to value transactions according to a standard definition. Export adjustments include counting military sales as services not goods, adding private gift parcels, and foreign official gold sales from U.S. private dealers. Import adjustments include adding in inland freight in Canada and foreign official gold sales to U.S. private dealers, and subtracting imports by U.S. military agencies.

a. Exports are valued on an f.a.s. basis, which refers to the free alongside ship value at the port of export and generally include inland freight, insurance, and other charges incurred in placing the goods alongside the carrier at the port of exportation.

b. Imports are valued as reported by the U.S. Customs Service, known as Customs basis, and exclude import duties, the cost of freight, insurance, and other charges incurred in bringing merchandise to the United States.

Table 2. U.S. Current Account Balances (billions of dollars)

Calendar Year	Merchandise Trade Balance[a]	Services Balance[b]	Investment Income Balance[c]	Net Unilateral Transfers[d]	Current Account Balance[e]
1985	-122.2	0.3	25.7	-22.0	-118.2
1986	-145.1	6.5	15.5	-24.1	-147.2
1987	-159.6	7.9	14.3	-23.3	-160.7
1988	-127.0	12.4	18.7	-25.3	-121.2
1989	-117.7	24.6	19.8	-26.2	-99.5
1990	-111.0	30.2	28.6	-26.7	-79.0
1991	-76.9	45.8	24.1	9.9	2.9
1992	-96.9	57.7	24.2	-35.1	-50.1
1993	-132.5	62.1	25.3	-39.8	-84.8
1994	-165.8	67.3	17.1	-40.3	-121.6
1995	-174.2	77.8	20.9	-38.1	-113.6
1996	-191.0	86.9	22.3	-43.0	-124.8
1997	-198.4	90.2	12.6	-45.1	-140.7
1998	-248.2	82.1	4.3	-53.2	-215.1
1999	-347.8	82.7	13.9	-50.4	-301.6
2000	-454.7	74.9	21.1	-58.6	-417.4
2001	-429.5	64.4	31.7	-51.3	-384.7
2002	-485.0	61.2	27.4	-64.9	-461.3
2003	-550.9	54.0	45.3	-71.8	-523.4
2004	-669.6	61.8	67.2	-84.5	-625.0
2005	-787.1	75.6	72.4	-89.8	-729.0
2006	-838.3	85.0	57.2	-92.0	-788.1
2007	-819.4	119.1	81.7	-112.7	-731.2
2008	—	—	—	—	—

Source: U.S. Bureau of Economic Analysis, U.S. International Transactions.

a. On a BoP basis.

b. Includes travel, transportation, fees and royalties, insurance payments, other government and private services, and investment income.

c. Income receipts on U.S. assets abroad minus income payments on foreign assets in the United States.

d. International transfers of funds, such as private gifts, pension payments, and government grants for which there is no quid pro quo.
e. The trade balance plus the service balance plus investment income balance plus net unilateral transfers, although conceptually equal to the current account balance, may differ slightly as a result of rounding.

FORECASTS

According to Global Insight, Inc., a leading U.S. economic forecasting firm, in 2008 the U.S. merchandise (goods) trade deficit is projected to decline to about $931.9 billion on a balance of payments basis and to stay at the level for 2009 and 2010 (see **Table 3** and **Figure 7**). The U.S. current account deficit declined from the peak of $811.5 billion in 2006 to $749.6 billion in 2007. The current account deficit is forecasted to increase to $763.6 billion 2008 and then to decrease in 2009 and 2010.

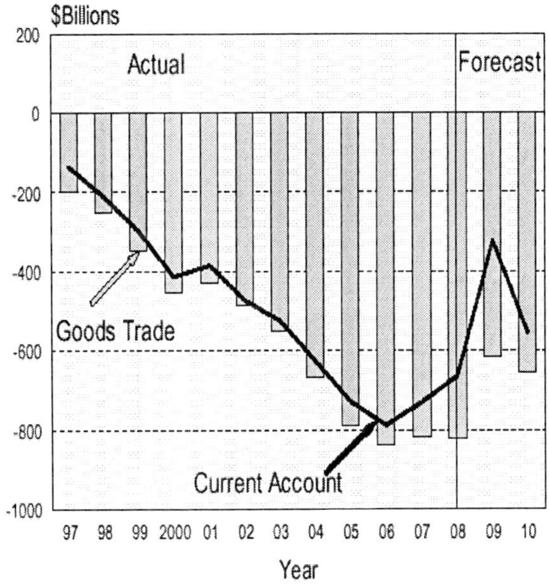

Sources: U.S. Bureau of Economic Analysis and Global Insight (BoP basis).

Figure 7. U.S. Merchandise Trade and Current Account Deficits, 1997-2010 (Forecast in Current Dollars)

Table 3. U.S. Merchandise and Current Account Trade, 2003 to 2010 (Forecast) (billions of U.S. dollars)

	2003	2004	2005	2006	2007	2008	2009	2010
Merchandise Trade								
Exports								
Actual	724.4	818.3	908.4	1032.1	1149.2	1291.3	—	—
Forecasted	—	—	—	—	—	—	1,035.1	1,025.0
Imports								
Actual	1284.0	1499.5	1705.3	1882.7	1985.2	2,112.5	—	—
Forecasted	—	—	—	—	—	—	1,489.9	1,661.9
Trade Balance								
Actual	-550.9	-669.6	-787.1	-838.3	-819.4	-821.2	—	—
Forecasted	—	—	—	—	—	—	-429.9	-581.8
Services Trade Balance								
Actual	54.0	61.8	75.6	85.0	119.1	—	—	—
Forecasted	—	—	—	—	—	147.4	165.2	175.1
Current Account Balance								
	2003	**2004**	**2005**	**2006**	**2007**	**2008**	**2009**	**2010**
Actual	-523.4	-625.0	-729.0	-788.1	-731.2	—	—	—
Forecasted	—	—	—	—	—	-679.7	-342.0	-489.0

Sources: U.S. Bureau of Economic Analysis and Global Insight (BoP basis).

U.S. Trade with Selected Nations

The overall U.S. merchandise trade balance consists of deficits or surpluses with each trading partner. Many economists view the overall figure as more significant than bilateral trade balances, since rising deficits with some nations are often offset by declining deficits or growing surpluses with others. Nonetheless, abnormally large or rapidly increasing trade deficits with particular countries are often viewed as indicators that underlying problems may exist with market access, the competitiveness of particular industries, currency misalignment, or macroeconomic adjustment. Figure 8 and Table 4 show U.S. trade balances with selected nations.

Most of the U.S. trade deficit can be accounted for by trade with China, Japan, Mexico, Canada, and Germany. Trade with the oil exporting countries, particularly Nigeria, Venezuela, and Saudi Arabia, also is in deficit. U.S. trade surpluses occur in trade with the Netherlands, Hong Kong, Australia, and the United Arab Emirates.

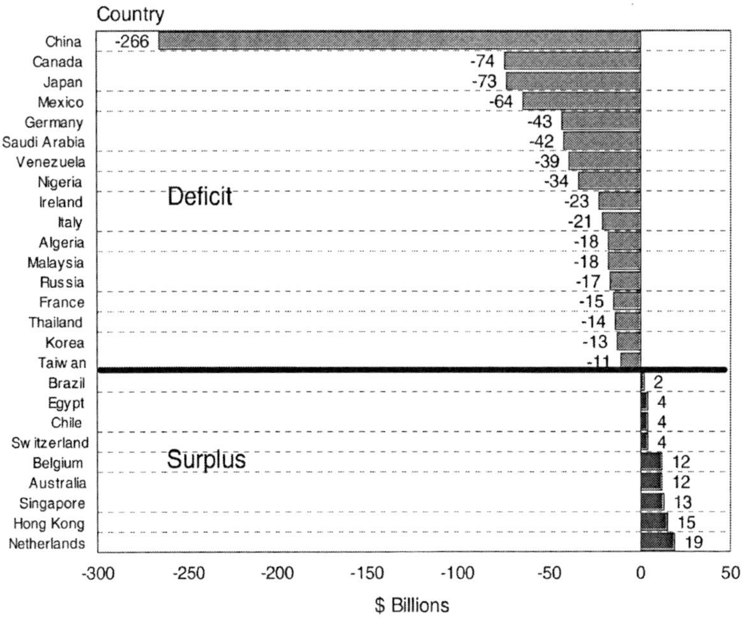

Source: CRS with data from the U.S. Department of Commerce (Census basis).

Figure 8. U.S. Merchandise Trade Balances With Selected Nations, 2008

The U.S. trade deficit with China has soared over the past decade. From $32 billion in 1995 to $100 billion in 2000 and $266 billion in 2008, the negative net balance in trade with China has grown to account for nearly 30% of the total U.S. trade deficit.[14] The U.S. trade deficit with China exceeded that with Japan for the first time in the year 2000 and now is more than three times as large.

China claims that its trade is less imbalanced than U.S. data indicate. Chinese trade data differ from those of the United States primarily because of the treatment of Hong Kong as an entrepot. Since Hong Kong is a separate customs area from mainland China, Beijing counts Hong Kong as the destination for its exports sent there, even though the goods may be transshipped to other markets. For example, China would count a laptop computer that is assembled in Shanghai but shipped through Hong Kong before being exported to the United States as a sale to Hong Kong. By contrast, the United States and many of China's other trading partners count Chinese exports that are transshipped through Hong Kong as products from China not Hong Kong, including goods that contain Hong Kong components or involve final packaging in Hong Kong. The United States also counts Hong Kong as the destination of U.S. products sent there, even those that are then reexported to China. However, the PRC counts many of such reexported goods as U.S. exports to China. So by U.S. figures, U.S. exports to China tend to be understated, while by Chinese figures, Chinese exports to the U.S. tend to be understated. The net result is that the trade surplus with the United States at $102 billion in 2008 that China reported is less than half the U.S. deficit with China of $266 billion reported by the United States.

Table 4. U.S. Merchandise Trade Balances with Selected Nations and Groups (millions of U.S. dollars, Census basis)

Country	2003	2004	2005	2006	2007	2008
Total	**-532,350**	**-650,930**	**-767,477**	**-817,304**	**-794,483**	**-821,153**
North America	-92,319	-111,547	-128,230	-136,056	-142,791	-138,550
Canada	-51,671	-66,480	-78,486	-71,782	-68,169	-74,174
Mexico	-40,648	-45,067	-49,744	-64,274	-74,622	-64,376
European Union	-98,521	-109,999	-123,123	-117,216	-107,168	-93,417
United Kingdom	-8,967	-10,274	-12,445	-8,103	-6,629	-4,844
Germany	-39,281	-45,850	-50,567	-47,763	-44,513	-42,821
France	-12,166	-10,342	-11,432	-12,822	-14,140	-14,810
Italy	-14,854	-17,413	-19,485	-20,109	-20,878	-20,665
Netherlands	9,742	11,839	11,623	13,787	14,560	40,223
Russia	-6,171	-8,930	-11,344	-15,127	-11,949	-17,440
Japan	-66,032	-75,562	-82,519	-88,568	-82,760	-72,669
China	-124,068	-161,938	-201,545	-232,589	-256,207	-266,333
Newly Industrialized Countries (NICS)	-21,217	-21,883	-15,782	-11,783	-3,904	3,758
Singapore	1,422	4,238	5,532	6,916	7,891	12,925
Hong Kong	4,669	6,513	7,459	9,829	13,092	15,149
Taiwan	-14,152	-12,879	-12,757	-15,165	-11,968	-11,048
S. Korea	-13,157	-19,755	-16,016	-13,362	-12,918	-13,269
South/Central American Countries	-26,883	-37,183	-50,460	-44,706	-27,345	-22,130
Argentina	-732	-357	-462	797	1,369	1,716
Brazil	-6,699	-7,263	-9,064	-7,136	-1,019	2,451
Colombia	-2,629	-2,751	-3,387	-2,557	-876	-1,654
OPEC	-51,064	-71,843	-92,867	-105,289	-112,987	-175,613
Venezuela	-14,305	-20,153	-27,557	-28,131	-29,709	-38,790
Saudi Arabia	-13,473	-15,702	-20,380	-24,049	-25,230	-42,308
Nigeria	-9,377	-14,694	-22,618	-25,630	-29,992	-33,966

Sources: United States Census Bureau, Foreign Trade Statistics. For other countries and further detail, see U.S. International Trade in Goods and Services Annual Revision for 2007, FT-900 (08-04), released June 10, 2008.

Table 5 lists the U.S. top deficit trading partners in merchandise trade, on a Census basis. In 2000, China overtook Japan as the top U.S. deficit trading partner. After, China, the next highest deficit trading partners are Japan, Mexico, Canada, Germany, and Nigeria.

Table 5. Top U.S. Merchandise Deficit Trading Partners, 2008 (millions of U.S. dollars)

Country	U.S. Balance	U.S. Exports	U.S. Imports
China	-266,333	71,457	337,790
Canada	-74,174	261,381	335,555
Japan	-72,669	66,579	139,248
Germany	-42,821	54,732	97,553
Saudi Arabia	-42,308	12,478	54,786
Venezuela	-38,790	12,611	51,401
Nigeria	-33,966	4,102	38,068
Ireland	-22,915	8,653	31,568
Italy	-20,665	15,479	36,143
Algeria	-18,112	1,243	19,355
Malaysia	-17,777	12,963	30,740
Russia	-17,440	9,335	26,775
France	-14,810	29,187	43,997
Thailand	-14,481	9,067	23,548
Korea	-13,269	34,807	48,076
Taiwan	-11,048	25,279	36,327
Indonesia	-9,886	5,913	15,799
Sweden	-7,405	5,084	12,489
India	-7,095	18,667	25,762
Austria	-5,821	2,649	8,471
United Kingdom	-4,844	53,775	58,619
Norway	-3,910	3,400	7,311
South Africa	-3,479	6,495	9,974
Finland	-2,145	3,762	5,906
Hungary	-1,698	1,431	3,129

Source: U.S. Department of Commerce. U.S. International Trade in Goods and Services, FT 900 (08-04).

Note: Data are on a Census basis. Exports are valued f.a.s.; imports are valued Customs.

Table 6 lists the United States' top trading partners ranked by trade turnover, defined as exports plus imports. As shown in Table 6, in 2008, as in 2007, Canada was America's largest total merchandise trading partner. Canada was followed by China, Mexico, Japan, Germany, the United Kingdom, Korea, Taiwan and France. Malaysia dropped from number 10 in total U.S. trade in 2006 to number 14 in 2007. Canada was the largest supplier of U.S. imports in 2006 and before, but in 2007 China surpassed Canada. By far, Canada is the top purchaser of U.S. exports with Mexico second. In 2007 China passed Japan to become third. Japan is now our fourth- ranked export market.

Table 6. Top U.S. Trading Partners Ranked by Total Merchandise Trade in 2008 (millions of U.S. dollars)

Rank	Country	Total Trade	U.S. Exports	U.S. Imports	Balance
1	Canada	596,936	261,381	335,555	-74,174
2	China	409,247	71,457	337,790	-266,333
3	Mexico	367,454	151,539	215,915	-64,376
4	Japan	205,827	66,579	139,248	-72,669
5	Germany	152,285	54,732	97,553	-42,821
6	United Kingdom	112,394	53,775	58,619	-4,844
7	Korea	82,883	34,807	48,076	-13,269
8	France	73,184	29,187	43,997	-14,810
9	Saudi Arabia	67,264	12,478	54,786	-42,308
10	Venezuela	64,012	12,611	51,401	-38,790
11	Brazil	63,369	32,910	30,459	2,451
12	Taiwan	61,606	25,279	36,327	-11,048
13	Netherlands	61,363	40,223	21,140	19,083
14	Italy	51,622	15,479	36,143	-20,664
15	Belgium	46,386	29,026	17,360	11,666
16	Singapore	44,694	28,810	15,884	12,926
17	India	44,429	18,667	25,762	-7,095
18	Malaysia	43,703	12,963	30,740	-17,777
19	Nigeria	42,170	4,102	38,068	-33,966
20	Ireland	40,221	8,653	31,568	-22,915
21	Switzerland	39,809	22,023	17,786	4,237
22	Russia	36,110	9,335	26,775	-17,440
23	Australia	33,039	22,457	10,582	11,875
24	Thailand	32,615	9,067	23,548	-14,481
25	Hong Kong	28,118	21,633	6,485	15,148

Source: U.S. Department of Commerce. *U.S. International Trade in Goods and Services*, FT 900 (08-04).

Notes: Total trade=imports + exports. Data are on a Census basis. Exports are valued f.a.s.; imports are valued Customs.

Table 7 lists trade balances on goods, services, and income, net unilateral transfers and current account balances for selected U.S. trading partners. While trade in services, flows of income from investments, and remittances home by foreign workers are considerably smaller than merchandise flows, as the economy has become more globalized and service-oriented, these components of the current account have become more important. In many cases, the bilateral current account balances are quite different from bilateral balances on merchandise trade only.

Table 7. U.S. Current Account Balances With Selected U.S. Trading Partners, 2007 (billions of U.S. dollars)

Country	Merchandise Trade Balance[a]	Services Balance[b]	Investment Income Balance[c]	Net Unilateral Transfers[d]	Current Account Balance[e]
All Countries	**-819.4**	**119.1**	**81.7**	**-112.7**	**-731.2**
Mexico	-77.6	8.0	1.6	-12.5	-80.5
Canada	-70.6	18.1	16.9	-1.7	-37.3
Asia and Pacific	**-410.3**	**33.1**	**-47.5**	**-21.0**	**-445.7**
China	-256.6	5.4	-36.1	-2.4	-289.7
Japan	-85.1	15.0	-41.2	1.2	-110.3
S. Korea	-13.9	4.8	-0.2	-0.6	-10.0
European Union	**-113.9**	**36.7**	**39.6**	**-4.7**	**-42.4**
Germany	-45.3	-6.0	1.2	-1.2	-51.2
United Kingdom	-7.6	16.5	-2.2	4.5	11.2
Latin America	**-105.3**	**22.8**	**27.1**	**-30.0**	**-85.5**
Middle East	**-33.8**	**0.1**	**-3.3**	**-12.0**	**-49.0**

Source: U.S. Bureau of Economic Analysis, International Transactions Account Data.

a. On a BoP basis.

b. Includes travel, transportation, fees and royalties, insurance payments, other government and private services, and investment income.

c. Income receipts on U.S. assets abroad minus income payments on foreign assets in the United States.

d. International transfers of funds, such as private gifts, pension payments, and government grants for which there is no *quid pro quo*.

e. The trade balance plus the service balance plus investment income balance plus net unilateral transfers, although equal to the current account balance, may differ as a result of rounding.

Country data for the current account are final for 2007 but not for 2008. Since Japan has invested considerable amounts in securities, equities, and in factories in the United States, the United States ran a deficit of $41.2 billion in investment income with that country in 2007. This more than offset the surplus of $15 billion in trade in services with Japan. As a result, the current account deficit with Japan of $110.3 billion in 2007 exceeded the bilateral merchandise trade deficit of $85.1 billion. Likewise with China; the U.S. deficit on investment income of $36.1 billion far overshadowed the U.S. surplus of $5.4 billion in services.

In 2007, a different situation existed with the European Union and Canada. The United States earned a $39.6 billion surplus in investment income with the EU in 2007, greater than 2006 investment income surplus of $12.6 billion. In 2007, the U.S. surplus in services with the EU came to $36.7 billion. These two flows offset a merchandise deficit of $113.9 billion to produce a U.S. current account deficit of $42.4 billion, lower than the 2006 current account deficit of $86.9 billion. From Canada the United States received $16.9 billion in investment income plus a surplus in services trade of $18.1 billion. Hence, the current account deficit with Canada at $37.3 billion was lower than the $70.6 billion merchandise trade deficit.

The rising deficit with many countries in investment income reflects the accumulating debt relative to the world of the United States. Inflows of capital to compensate for the U.S. trade deficit and low U.S. savings rate help to maintain the value of the dollar, but interest paid and other income that accrues to that capital is often repatriated to the home countries. That means more capital must be invested in the United States or the United States must export more to compensate for the outflows of investment income. In 2007, the overall U.S. balance on investment income registered a surplus of $81.7 billion, higher than the 2006 balance on investment income of $57.2 billion. Imbalances in investment income with certain countries have been growing and could become a problem in the future.

ADVANCED TECHNOLOGY, AUTOS, AND OIL

Table 8 shows U.S. trade in advanced technology products. This includes about 500 commodity classification codes representing products whose technology is from a recognized high technology field (e.g., biotechnology) or that represent the leading technology in a field. The United States long ran a surplus in these products, but that surplus dropped sharply in 2000 and turned into a deficit in 2002. The U.S. trade balance in high technology products was last in surplus in 2001.

In 2002 to 2005, the U.S. ran a trade deficit in high technology products which grew roughly ten billion dollars per year, from $16.6 billion to $43.6 billion. In 2006 this deficit dropped to $38.1 billion, but in 2007 resumed its former path of growing ten billion dollars per year, to $52.6 billion, but in 2008, this deficit grew to only $55.5 billion. This deficit does not necessarily imply that the United States is losing the high technology race, since many of the high technology imports are from U.S. companies (particularly electronics manufacturers) who assemble the products overseas. However, this growing deficit may warrant closer policy scrutiny.

Table 8. U.S. Trade in Advanced Technology Products (billions of U.S. dollars)

Year	U.S. Exports	U.S. Imports	Trade Balance
1990	93.4	59.3	34.1
1995	138.4	124.8	13.6
1996	154.9	130.4	24.5
1997	179.5	147.3	32.2
1998	186.4	156.8	29.6
1999	200.3	181.2	19.1
2000	227.4	222.1	5.3
2001	200.1	195.3	4.8
2002	178.6	195.2	-16.6
2003	180.2	207.0	-26.8
2004	201.4	238.3	-36.9
2005	216.1	259.7	-43.6
2006	252.7	290.8	-38.1
2007	275.8	326.8	-52.6
2008	275.8	331.4	-55.5

Source: U.S. Bureau of the Census. *U.S. International Trade in Goods and Services*. FT-900, issued monthly.

Notes: Includes about 500 of some 22,000 commodity classification codes that meet the following criteria: (1) contains products whose technology is from a recognized high technology field (e.g., biotechnology), (2) represent leading edge technology in that field, and (3) constitute a significant part of all items covered in the selected classification code. Data are on a BoP basis.

Table 9 provides data on trade in passenger cars with major automobile producing nations for 2008. This does not include foreign cars assembled in the United States. The United States incurs the largest deficits in this trade with Japan, Mexico, Germany, South Korea, and Canada. The U.S. trade balance in motor vehicles improved from a $144,990 million deficit in 2006 to a $120,941 million deficit in 2007, but declined to a $107,065 deficit in 2008.[15]

Table 10 shows imports of crude petroleum by major country source. In 2007, the United States imported $246 billion in crude oil or 13% of all imports. Roughly half comes from the Organization of the Petroleum Exporting Countries (OPEC) with Saudi Arabia, Venezuela, and Nigeria the predominant suppliers. Imports from Iraq are recovering with $11 billion worth in 2007. Over 40% of U.S. petroleum imports come from non-OPEC sources, primarily Canada and Mexico.[16]

Table 9. U.S. Trade in Motor Vehicles (Passenger Cars, Trucks, and Buses) and Parts by Selected Countries, 2008 (millions of U.S. dollars)

Trading Partner	U.S. Exports	U.S. Imports	Trade Balance
TOTAL	125,839	232,904	-107,065
Japan	2,235	55,784	-53,549
Mexico	19,228	48,273	-29,045
Germany	10,387	25,975	-15,588
Korea	855	11,354	-10,499
United Kingdom	2,275	5,166	-2,891
Taiwan	127	2,138	-2,011
Sweden	470	1,955	-1,485
Austria	418	1,791	-1,373
Brazil	1,000	1,812	-812
Belgium	790	987	-197
Canada	54,110	53,599	511
Australia	2,410	1,039	1,371
Saudi Arabia	3,764	7	3,757
Other	27,770	23,023	4,747

Source: U.S. Bureau of the Census, *U.S. International Trade in Goods and Services*, FT-900 (08-04).

Table 10. U.S. Imports of Crude Oil from Selected Countries, 2007 (quantity and customs value)

Country	Customs Value ($ million)	Quantity (thousand barrels)
Total World	**245,771**	**3,812,663**
OPEC Total	145,839	2,190,303
Saudi Arabia	33,870	516,375
Venezuela	32,143	517,179
Nigeria	30,882	417,672
Algeria	14,506	204,636
Angola	12,130	182,999
Iraq	10,874	171,628
Ecuador	4,360	71,611
Kuwait	3,754	61,725
Libya	2,612	35,698
Indonesia	474	7,475
United Arab Emirates	233	3,307
Qatar	0	0
Iran	0	0
Non-OPEC Total	**99,932**	**1,622,359**
Canada	38,330	660,738
Mexico	30,523	507,066
Brazil	3,761	59,719
Colombia	3,548	51,822
Russia	3,169	45,287
Congo	2,895	40,974
United Kingdom	2,543	36,464
Chad	2,107	35,858
Gabon	2,099	30,127
Other Non-OPEC	10,957	154,304

Sources: U.S. Census Bureau, *U.S. International Trade in Goods and Services*, FT-900, issued monthly, and World Trade Atlas, using Harmonized Schedule (HS) 270900 for crude oil.

Note: Census basis data.

Some Common Perceptions

This section of the report addresses a few common perceptions about trade that can be validated by data.

Is the Trade Deficit at a Dangerous Level?

The International Monetary Fund has used its experience with currency and exchange rate crises to say that caution should be exercised when a nation's current account deficit reaches a level of 5% of gross domestic product. At this level, nations have difficulty borrowing to finance imports and the nation's exchange rate may come under severe downward pressure. The United States is a special case, since the dollar is a secondary medium of exchange (one can use dollars in many foreign countries without exchanging them for local currency) and dollars are used extensively as an official reserve currency by national banks. Still, the IMF has been warning that the size of the U.S. current account deficit could cause a large depreciation of the dollar and disrupt financial markets. In the current global financial crisis, the dollar and U.S. Treasury securities are being viewed as a safe haven for investors, so capital inflows into the United States have remained sufficient to cover U.S. budget deficits and other government borrowing.

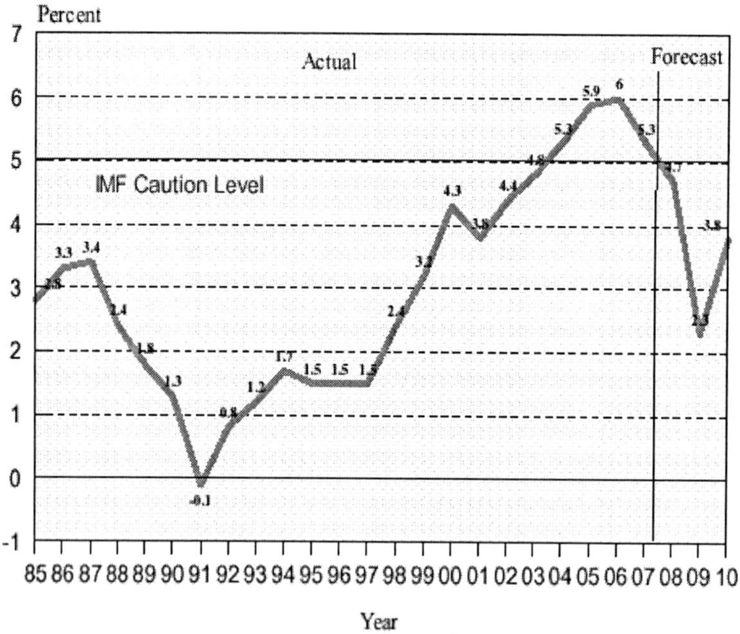

Sources: Data from U.S. Department of Commerce. Forecasts by Global Insight, Inc.

Figure 9.The U.S. Current Account Deficit as a Percent of Gross Domestic Product, 1985-2010 (forecast)

Figure 9 shows the U.S. current account balance as a percent of nominal U.S. gross domestic product (GDP). It grew in magnitude from near zero in 1980 to 3.4% in 1987, dropped into negative 0.1% in 1991 and rose to 6% in 2006 (exceeding the 5% level considered to warrant caution by the International Monetary Fund). The current account balance-GDP ratio remained above the IMF caution level for 2007 at 5.3%. However, beginning in 2008 through 2010, it is forecast to decline to below the IMF caution level primarily because the U.S. recession is shrinking imports faster than exports and causing the trade deficit to decline. This effect is expected to continue through 2009 before it begins to rise again in 2010.

IS TRADE WITH CHINA MERELY REPLACING THAT WITH SOUTHEAST ASIA?

Some observers claim that the rising U.S. imports from China are merely displacing those from other East Asian nations. Labor intensive industries, such as apparel, shoes, and consumer electronics, that produce for export to the United States and other industrialized nations are simply moving to China from Southeast Asian nations, including South Korea, and Taiwan. The overall level of imports from Asia is not changing. Its composition is just shifting toward China.

For specific industries, the shift in imports from traditional Asian exporting nations to China is clear. In woven apparel (HS 62), for example, in 1990, Hong Kong, South Korea, and Taiwan accounted for 33.4% of U.S. imports as compared to China with a 14.7% share. By 2006, China accounted for 35.3% of such imports, as compared to 4.9% for Hong Kong, South Korea, and Taiwan combined. In 2007, China's contribution to U.S. imports of woven apparel increased to 35.7%. Hong Kong, South Korea, and Taiwan collectively represented 3.4% of such imports, a decline from 2006.[17] The decline in woven apparel imports from Hong Kong, South Korea, and Taiwan also may reflect their shift to production of high-technology goods. As these Southeast Asian countries continue to industrialize, woven apparel imports from less-developed countries, such as Indonesia, Bangladesh, and Vietnam, likely will continue to increase.

Table 11. Changes in U.S. Merchandise Trade Balances With Selected Countries and Groups, 2006 and 2007

Country	2005	2006	2007	% Chg 2006/2005	% Chg 2007/2006
World Total	-$767,477	-$817,304	-$794,483	6.5	-2.8
China	-$201,545	-$232,589	-$256,207	15.4	10.2
-OPEC-	-$104,217	-$119,825	-$127,414	15.0	6.3
-EU 27-	**-$123,123**	**-$117,216**	**-$107,167**	**-4.8**	**-8.6**
Japan	-$82,519	-$88,568	-$82,760	7.3	**-6.6**
Mexico	-$49,744	-$64,274	-$74,622	29.2	16.1
Canada	-$78,486	-$71,782	-$68,169	**-8.5**	**-5.0**
Germany	-$50,567	-$47,763	-$44,513	**-5.6**	**-6.8**
Nigeria	-$22,618	-$25,630	-$29,992	13.3	17.0
Venezuela	-$27,557	-$28,131	-$29,709	2.1	5.6
Saudi Arabia	-$20,380	-$24,049	-$25,230	18.0	4.9
Malaysia	-$23,224	-$23,989	-$20,948	3.3	**-12.7**
Algeria	-$9,279	-$14,354	-$16,164	54.7	12.6
Thailand	-$12,633	-$14,320	-$14,300	13.4	-0.1
France	-$11,432	-$12,822	-$14,140	12.2	10.3
Hong Kong	$7,459	$9,829	$13,092	31.8	33.2
Korea, South	-$16,016	-$13,362	-$12,918	**-16.6**	**-3.3**
Taiwan	-$12,757	-$15,165	-$11,968	18.9	**-21.1**
Russia	-$1 1,344	-$15,127	-$11,949	33.4	**-21.0**
Asian 4 NICs	-$15,782	-$11,783	-$3,904	**-25.3**	**-66.9**

Source: U.S. Department of Commerce, Bureau of the Census via World Trade Atlas.

Notes: Merchandise trade data on a Census Basis. The U.S. balance with Hong Kong is positive. Members of OPEC are listed in, above. Members of Asian 4 Newly Industrializing Countries (NICs) are: Hong Kong, Singapore, South Korea and Taiwan.

In terms of overall imports, however, U.S. imports from Hong Kong, Taiwan, and South Korea rose from $50.6 billion (10.2% of total U.S. imports) in 1990 to $92.9 billion (4.7% of total) in 2007, while imports from China rose from $15.2 billion (3.3% of total) in 1990 to $321.4 billion (16.4% of total) in 2007.[18] Clearly, the share of U.S. imports from Hong Kong, Taiwan, and South Korea has been falling, while the share of imports from China is rising. The value of U.S. imports from both, however, continues to rise, while the value of those from China is rising faster.

The large U.S. trade deficit with China, moreover, is not just a transfer of the deficit from other Asian nations to China. The U.S. trade deficit with Hong Kong, Taiwan, and South Korea has gone from $17.9 billion (17.5% of the total U.S. deficit) in 1990 to $11.8 billion (1.5% of the total) in 2007. U.S. trade with Hong Kong actually went from a deficit in 1992 to a surplus in 1993, and has remained in surplus through 2007. The U.S. trade deficit with China, meanwhile, went from $10.4 billion (10.2% of the total U.S. trade deficit) in 1990 to $256.2 billion (32.2% of the total) in 2007. What actually is happening is quite complex. While the U.S. trade deficit with the world is declining, it continues to rise with China, Mexico and oil exporting countries. Table 11 illustrates this complexity. Negative percentage change numbers, noted in bold, indicate a shrinking U.S. merchandise trade deficit with that country or group. Positive percentage changes indicate growing deficits.

INTERNATIONAL TRADE STATISTICS WEB RESOURCES

Listed below are a list of resources available online for international trade statistics.

The single most authoritative, comprehensive, and frequently-published trade data statistical source is the monthly "FT900". Its actual title is *U.S. International Trade in Goods and Services*. The FT-900 is issued monthly by the U.S. Census Bureau and the U.S. Bureau of Economic Analysis. It provides information on the U.S. trade in goods and services (balance, exports, and imports) in specific commodities and end-use categories and with selected countries. The report also provides information on trade in advanced technology, petroleum, and motor vehicle products. The report is available from the U.S. Bureau of Economic Analysis at *http://www.bea.gov/ news releases/rels.htm*. Under "International" click on latest news release.

Information on trade in specific commodities, with particular regions, or for different time periods also can be obtained from the U.S. International Trade Commission at http://dataweb.usitc.gov/ (registration is required).

Historical and current U.S. exchange rate data are available from the Federal Reserve Bank of St. Louis at http://research.stlouisfed.org/fred2/.

End Notes

[1] Monthly trade data are available from the U.S. Bureau of Economic Analysis at http://www.bea.gov/newsreleases/ International/trade/2008/pdf/trad0808.pdf.

[2] See, for example, CRS Report RL3 1832, *The Export Administration Act: Evolution, Provisions, and Debate*, by Ian F. Fergusson; CRS Report RL33550, *Trade Remedy*

Legislation: Applying Countervailing Action to Nonmarket Economy Countries, by Vivian C. Jones; CRS Report RL32014, *WTO Dispute Settlement: Status of U.S. Compliance in Pending Cases*, by Jeanne J. Grimmett; CRS Report RL3 3274, *Financing the U.S. Trade Deficit*, by James K. Jackson; CRS Report RL33 867, *Tariff Modifications: Miscellaneous Tariff Bills*, by Vivian C. Jones; or CRS Report RL3 1032, *The U.S. Trade Deficit: Causes, Consequences, and Cures*, by Craig K. Elwell.

[3] Commerce Department data are available at http://www.bea.gov/.

[4] U.S. International Trade Commission data are available at http://dataweb.usitc.gov/.

[5] For further information on trade deficits and the macroeconomy, see CRS Report RL3 1032, *The U.S. Trade Deficit: Causes, Consequences, and Cures*, by Craig K. Elwell and CRS Report RL33 186, *Is the U.S. Current Account Deficit Sustainable?*, by Marc Labonte.

[6] U.S. trade in goods and services plus net flows of investment income and remittances.

[7] Statistics on Japanese international reserves are released on a monthly basis by the Japanese Ministry of Finance and available at https://www.mof.go.jp/english/.

[8] Statistics on Chinese international reserves are available from the Chinability website, a non-profit website that provides Chinese economic and business data and analysis, at http://www.chinability.com/.

[9] Statistics on foreign holdings of U.S. Treasury securities are available at http://www.treasury.gov/tic/mfh.txt. For further information, seeCRS Report RS2233 1, *Foreign Holdings of Federal Debt*, by Justin Murray and Marc Labonte.

[10] For more information on sovereign wealth funds, see CRS Report RL34336, *Sovereign Wealth Funds: Background and Policy Issues for Congress*, by Martin A. Weiss, CRS Report RL34337, *China's Sovereign Wealth Fund*, by Michael F. Martin.

[11] See Mann, Catherine L. *Is the U.S. Trade Deficit Sustainable?* Washington, Institute for International Economics, 1999. 224 p. See also:CRS Report RL33274, *Financing the U.S. Trade Deficit*, by James K. Jackson.CRS Report RL3 1032, *The U.S. Trade Deficit: Causes, Consequences, and Cures*, by Craig K. Elwell.

[12] For details, seeCRS Report RS20826, *Structure and Functions of The Federal Reserve System*, by Pauline Smale.

[13] For legislation related to trade with China and the Chinese currency, seeCRS Report RL33536, *China-U.S. Trade Issues*, by Wayne M. Morrison.

[14] For details and policy discussion, see CRS Report RL33536, *China-U.S. Trade Issues*, by Wayne M. Morrison.

[15] For information on the automobile industry, seeCRS Report RL32883, *U.S. Automotive Industry: Recent History and Issues*, by Stephen Cooney and Brent D. Yacobucci.

[16] For policy discussion, seeCRS Report RS22204, *U.S. Trade Deficit and the Impact of Rising Oil Prices*, by James K. Jackson.

[17] Calculations based on data from World Trade Atlas, using HS 62 for woven apparel.

[18] The numbers are comparable for all Asian countries.

CHAPTER SOURCES

The following chapters have been previously published:

Chapter 1 – This is an edited, excerpted and augmented edition of a United States Congressional Research Service publication, Report Order Code R40167, dated January 16, 2009.

Chapter 2 – This is an edited, excerpted and augmented edition of a United States Congressional Research Service publication, Report Order Code R40461, dated March 23, 2009.

Chapter 3 – This is an edited, excerpted and augmented edition of a United States Congressional Research Service publication, Report Order Code RL33577, dated March 6, 2009.

INDEX

D

E

F

G

H

I

J

K

L

M

P

Q

R

T

U

V

W